40¢ 55

MINISTERING
TO THE
PHYSICALLY SICK

PRENTICE-HALL, INC., ENGLEWOOD CLIFFS, N.J.

MINISTERING
TO THE
PHYSICALLY SICK

CARL J. SCHERZER

Ministering to the Physically Sick, by Carl J. Scherzer

Prentice-Hall, International, Inc.
(*London, Tokyo, Sydney, Paris*)
Prentice-Hall of Canada, Ltd.
Prentice-Hall de Mexico, S.A.

Printed in the United States of America

To Virginia

"But for you who fear my name the sun of righteousness shall rise, with healing in its wings."   *Malachi* 4:2

INTRODUCTION

This series of books represents the most comprehensive publishing effort ever made in the field of pastoral care. These books could not have been published twenty-five years ago, or probably even ten, for the material was not then available. In the past, single books have been available covering different phases of the task. Now we are bringing the subjects together in a single series. Here we present a library of pastoral care covering the major topics and problems that most pastors will encounter in their ministry. Fortunately, not all of these problems need be faced every week or even every month. But, when they are, the minister wants help and he wants it immediately.

These books are prepared for the non-specialized minister serving the local church, where he is the most accessible professional person in the community. It is a well accepted fact that more people turn to clergy when in trouble than to all other professional people. Therefore, the pastor must not fail them.

Russell L. Dicks,
General Editor

PREFACE

Religious people are not immune from spiritual problems. Believers cannot be expected to ignore spiritual difficulties simply because they are urged to do so or because they are reassured that God loves them. Many people must be helped to live with their problems and to use them creatively. Spiritual equilibrium or adjustment can be achieved amid perplexing and painful experiences when God's redemptive forces are personally appropriated.

The minister who is spiritually, mentally and emotionally mature can render effective help to people with definite problems induced by sickness. Part I relates to the pastor's personal growth and the spiritual deficits and resources that he can use in applying spiritual therapy to the sick.

Through the efforts of social scientists new information is constantly being made available to the minister regarding the nature of man and his reactions to his environment. The minister can appropriate these new insights and concepts to improve his skill in applying spiritual therapy to those who are in need of it.

The Bible speaks to every human need. The clergyman who is adequately prepared to read it intelligently, study it diligently, and permit God's Holy Spirit to guide him in the understanding of it will find it to be one of the most affective sources for the application of guidance and reassurance to a troubled person.

We have barely begun to understand the subjective and objective values of prayer. From experience we know that it is our greatest privilege. God is the source of all healing forces. Through sincere prayer, God lends His spirit to human needs in whatever manner it may be beneficial for man's spiritual welfare, either temporal or eternal.

This book is written to aid the parish clergyman in his ministry to the sick. The term "sick" is used in reference to physical ailments and "ill" or "illness" as man's emotional and spiritual reaction to sickness. A neurotic, for example, is ill but may not be sick. Many people can adjust to sickness without becoming ill.

All the case studies and examples are from the parish ministry except those otherwise indicated. Some are from my experience as a parish pastor and others are from case studies submitted to me by ministerial students, either written or verbal.

I owe a deep debt of gratitude to Dr. Russell L. Dicks, under whose guidance I received clinical training and to whom I submitted case studies for criticism for a number of years. To Dr. Albert G. Hahn, Mrs. Clara Zuspann, William D. Lightfoot, Virginia Scherzer, and to the thousands of patients, doctors, clergy and nurses who have helped me in any way I am sincerely thankful. The Apostle Paul expressed it best when he wrote, "And for everything giving thanks in the name of our Lord Jesus Christ to God the Father." (Eph. 5: 20)

CONTENTS

MINISTERING
TO THE
PHYSICALLY SICK

PART I

THE PASTOR

AND THE NATURE

OF ILLNESS

ONE

The PASTOR'S DEMEANOR

INTRODUCTION

A minister was praying with a middle-aged woman parishioner who was a patient in the hospital. "Dear Lord," he said in the prayer, "heal this Your faithful servant. You know how badly she is needed in the church and such a saint can do so much good for Your kingdom. . . ."

I was not eavesdropping. The minister was praying so loudly that I heard him as I started to enter the room. I waited in the corridor until he finished, then, as he left, he hastened past me.

Entering, I first introduced myself to the other patient in the room although I was a bit curious to meet the "saint."

When I came to her bedside I mentioned that I had heard her pastor praying with her.

With a sheepish grin she said, "I wish I were half as good as he thinks I am."

"Is that so?" I asked responding with a smile.

"Do you have time to listen?" she asked.

"Yes, I do," I said, pulling a chair near the bed for I sensed she wanted to express some feelings of guilt.

I drew the curtain for privacy and she proceeded to tell her story. To make it brief, she secretly desired a man who sings in the choir with her and went so far as to travel to another city to be with him. There she registered at the same hotel where he was staying. To bolster her courage she bought a pint of whisky and drank some of it mixed with water. Unaccustomed to liquor, she became intoxicated and fell asleep. When she awoke just before dawn she was so nauseated that she was in no mood to call his room. That very morning she took a bus back home and the man never learned about the

17

"affair." She did purchase a few items because she had told her husband that she was going to that city to do some shopping.

As we discussed her guilt feelings I asked if she had ever gone to her pastor for help.

"Oh, for heaven's sake no," was her quick response. With apprehension she added, "And I hope you will never tell him."

I reassured her on that point of confidence, and she was at ease again. When I asked her why she would not confide in him she gave the following reasons:

"He is so busy that he wouldn't have time to listen to my problems."

"I'm afraid he would mention it in a sermon."

"He's not the kind of person I'd talk to about such things. He'd think I'm terrible and it would be a disgrace if he asked me to quit the choir."

Much has been written on the pastoral techniques in counseling the sick, but little attention has been given to the importance of the acceptance by the patient of the pastor as counselor. No matter how skilled he may be in counseling, his demeanor will determine the extent to which people will confidently accept his ministration.

Poise

One important phase of the pastor's demeanor is his poise. We describe poise as composure, steadiness, and mental, emotional and spiritual maturity. Many of the pastor's people who are sick look to him for spiritual and emotional support. He can instill such confidence only if he has the required poise.

It is a tremendous responsibility to help a mother accept with faith the suffering or death of her child. Nor is it much easier to understand why a calamity should befall an aged, helpless person or a person in middle age who is so badly needed by the family.

The pastor may not have ready answers to all the deep and troubling questions that arise in suffering and death. There is no easy formula that can be applied in each instance. The doctor can administer a certain drug to combat an identified disease. The pastor cannot. Every person is an individual who needs specialized spiritual therapy. However, the minister with poise communicates his faith and stability to the troubled.

The Busy Pastor

When the minister either purposely or inadvertently leaves the impression that he is too busy to hear his parishioners' troubles, few will have the temerity to interrupt his busy schedule. The woman gave that as one of the reasons why she did not come to her pastor with her problem. When parishioners know that their pastor is not too busy to listen to their needs, they call upon him for help in time of need.

Emotional and Spiritual Maturation

Another important phase of the pastor's poise is his emotional and spiritual maturity. A minister's nine-year-old daughter passed away on a Saturday morning. As soon as the news of it spread through the congregation there was an outpouring of sympathy for him and his wife. The president of the congregation, with a few of the members of the official Church Board, called upon him that afternoon. In kindness they told him that the members would understand if there was no service the next day.

The pastor kindly explained that he would proceed with the worship service as usual. Of course, he felt keenly the earthly loss of their child but he did not "sorrow as those who have no hope."

"I preach the importance of faith in God and now I want to witness to it," he said. "I know that our dear child is with our Lord, and I would have no excuse to offer Him for refusing to preach His Gospel tomorrow."

Such a demonstration of his own faith served to confirm the faith of his people more than did his sermon the next day. The spiritual maturity of the pastor is communicated through his poise.

Ethics

The pastor's ethics are also an important phase of his poise. The woman said that she was afraid that he might mention it in a sermon.

If the pastor is to have the confidence of his people he must be careful not to discuss a specific problem of a parishioner in a sermon except by permission of the person involved. Even then, no names should be mentioned and the congregation might be told that permission has been granted to use the illustration. The temptation to use such confidential material should be avoided whenever possible. The resourceful pastor has ample supply of illustrations in Scripture, religious literature, and previous parish experience elsewhere.

The pastor's ethics also relates to what he may reveal to others in private conversations. A fourteen-year-old girl took an overdose of sleeping pills and she was hospitalized in a single room. Her pastor called on her and, as he was leaving, the father of another child who knew the minister asked him, "What is the matter with that girl?" In what I hope was an unguarded moment, the minister told him. When this man started to discuss the girl's problem with her parents they were justifiably angry with their pastor for telling it. It is doubtful if the parents of the girl will confide in that pastor again.

The minister may often be placed in an embarrassing position when individuals ask him to reveal the nature of another person's sickness. In all such instances he must be guarded in his response. Truthfully he may say that he does not know all the details of the sickness and suggest that the inquirer ask a member of the family of the patient or the attending physician. Many of the patients do not want the nature of their sickness discussed by others.

In connection with the pastor's ethics he may be urged by certain members of his congregation to call upon a friend or a relative affiliated with another church. In such instances he may inquire if the patient's pastor is visiting him and suggest that it would be embarrassing if both pastors were to call at the same time. This impasse often happens and the sick one's pastor does not know whether to "break into" the visit on his call or not to call at all. The pastor has no more right to call upon another's parishioner than a doctor has to call upon another's patient. When the pressure upon him is too heavy he may make a social call upon the sick one as others do and explain to the patient that a relative or friend, whichever it might be, asked him to say a word of greeting in passing.

Preserving the dignity of his pastoral office is an ethical phase of his demeanor that leaves a favorable impression upon his people.

Understanding Human Nature

Another factor that contributes to his poise is the pastor's understanding of human nature. As he matures emotionally he becomes less prone to make judgments. Generally speaking, young ministers may be more opinionated than older, more experienced ones.

Sam Jones was a middle-aged bachelor member of the church. He gladly donated his services for decorating the church or the parish hall and could be depended upon to give physical labor when it was needed. But Sam never attended a church service! The young minister urged him to come to church, but to no avail. Sam would smile and say that he would come sometime, but he never did and the young pastor blamed him for it.

"You can find time to go to the theater," the young pastor said impatiently one day to him. "It seems to me that if you had any interest in the Kingdom of God you'd make it your business to be there. If all the members were like you we'd have to close the church doors."

Sometime later Sam became seriously ill. The day previous to surgery, when the minister called upon him in the hospital, he said, "Reverend, I wonder if you would bring me Communion. I haven't had the Lord's supper since I was confirmed."

"Would you like to have Communion now?" the pastor asked.

"If it is convenient with you," he responded.

As the minister went to his car to get the Communion kit, he was puzzled. If Sam wanted Communion now, why did he not attend the Lord's Table previously in the Church?

When he returned to Sam's bedside, he said, "How is it, Sam, that you have not Communed all these years?"

This was the first effort on the part of this young minister to understand Sam's problem. Given this opportunity, Sam confided in him. When he was confirmed he was the only boy in the class who did not get a new suit of clothes. His parents could not afford it and some of the other boys made snide remarks about him. Children can be very cruel at times and Sam was embarrassed. He went through with Confirmation because of parental pressure. Then he went home to his room and cried. Thereafter, his parents could not make him go to church because he used the incident as an excuse that others would ridicule him. This attitude may have contributed to the development of a latent fear of people caused by previous experiences of inadequacy and inferiority. He never married. He could attend a theater because it was dark within. In a lighted area with many people he became panicky.

If Sam could have had adequate understanding and assistance earlier in life, it would have helped him to overcome his fear of people. After this conversation the minister could appreciate Sam's problem and rightfully blamed himself for judging too hastily. With sympathetic understanding the minister could support Sam with Christian love.

The woman expressed her fear of her pastor's judgmental attitude when she said, "He'd think I am terrible and it would be a disgrace if he asked me to quit the choir."

When the minister understands human nature to the extent that he can tolerate its foibles and tricks without losing his emotional equilibrium, his people soon learn that they need not fear him and are able to discuss any problem with him. They will trust him to listen and to guide them with sympathetic understanding.

In most instances of nonconformity or unusual moral behavior the pastor can be fairly certain that the person has been previously conditioned by some traumatic experience. Some of these incidents occur in childhood and even in infancy. While the minister is not adequately trained to be a psychiatrist, he can be understanding in his relationships with his people and they will respond by offering him their confidence.

Friendliness

The minister's demeanor reflects phases of his personality other than poise. His friendliness also makes him approachable. His sincere love for people expresses itself in a friendly attitude. Every person, including pastors, has a toleration point in any given emotional area beyond which it is very difficult for him to emanate friendliness. He may, for example, become irritated by criticism and in an unguarded moment speak disparingly about his critic. On the contrary, he may make a definite effort to emotionally adjust to the criticism without hostility or resentment. He may channel the criticism constructively, utilizing it for self-improvement.

The minister's emotional maturity reflects itself in friendliness toward all his people, including his known critics. Aware that a person does not like him, he may overlook the attitude and still be friendly without being too aggressive. If he permits the unfriendly attitude to disturb him or cause him to go to extremes in being kind or in praising the hostile one, these expressions will be harmful to both. He may worry about his own insincerity and cause the offending one to be more unfriendly and proud that the minister makes such an effort to gain approval. Normally, the minister can be friendly in any situation and still retain the dignity of his office.

Attire

The minister's attire, personal hygiene and voice are also attributes of his demeanor. While the minister need not dress as if he were in perpetual mourning when he visits the sick, neither is it advisable to appear in sport clothes. Clothes do not make the man, but they do contribute, in a measure, to the manner in which he is received by those upon whom he calls. Conservative and neat attire makes a favorable impression on the sick. Such attire unconsciously leaves the impression that he intends the call to be important and respects the one whom he is visiting.

Personal Hygiene

Regarding personal hygiene the pastor must be careful about odors emanating from his person. The olfactory nerves of the sick one may be hypersensitive. To a nauseated person even the odor of after-shave lotion may be offensive.

The Voice

In the beginning of this chapter I mentioned that the minister was praying so loudly that he could be heard in the outside hall. During sickness the auditory nerves may also be hypersensitive, so much so that the slightest noise may annoy the patient with a headache.

The minister may cultivate his speaking voice so that it is pleasant to hear, not unduly loud nor so soft that the patient must strain to hear him.

One minister explained that he prays with his patients in a loud voice so that his witness to the Lord would reach out to other patients in the room. His intentions may be worthy, but in all probability his loud voice will have the opposite effect upon those who are annoyed by it. His intent also detracts from his personal interest in the one whom he is visiting. The patient will know that the prayer is not meant to be personal but for the benefit of any other person who might hear it. This may be very annoying, even more so if the patient has suggested certain requests to be included in the prayer.

When there are other patients in the room, they may be of different faiths and prefer a priest, a rabbi or another pastor to pray with them. In one such instance, recently, the second patient in the room was of the Roman Catholic faith. When the two patients returned home they communicated with each other by phone. Some time later, the Catholic patient had to return to the hospital and evidently told her Protestant friend who relayed the information to her pastor. He took it upon himself to visit her in the hospital.

"I didn't mind his coming to see me," she said. "I appreciated that. But he came almost every day. I let him pray for me a few times and then I thought I'd better tell him that I'd rather he wouldn't. I hate to be rude to him, but now I wish he would let me alone." This pastor would have been helpful to her if he had respected her faith and refrained from calling upon her.

Fortunately there is a happy medium between the loud voice and the one that is too soft to be heard. As a singing voice is developed by practice, the minister can also learn to control his voice so that it will communicate confidence and kindness without affectation.

ESTABLISHING RAPPORT

Through Preaching

The pastor's demeanor will, to a large extent, determine the measure of rapport with his parishioners.

Indirectly he may elicit a friendly sympathetic relationship through his preaching. On occasion he may encourage confidence by saying that as a pastor he does not reveal to anyone anything that is told to him in confidence. He may suggest that he is not too busy to listen to the problems of his people and is available for counseling by appointment. Using some of the healing miracles of Jesus for sermonizing he may discuss the significance of the pastoral sick call.

Empathy

A minister can seldom be helpful to a person who dislikes him, or who reluctantly comes to him under pressure unless he can first achieve empathy. Occasions arise when he is urged to step into strained family situations uninvited by those who are involved. In all such situations the pastor may make himself available, but when the counselees will not extend to him their confidence he is at a distinct disadvantage.

The family doctor of an unmarried lady told her pastor that she "has nothing wrong with her. If she'd stop thinking about herself and start doing something for other people she wouldn't be sick all the time. If you want to help her, you tell her, Reverend."

The inexperienced young pastor followed the doctor's advice. The physician's diagnosis might have been correct but his suggested therapy was not. Seeking only to be helpful the young pastor told her as gently as he could what the physician had said. She reacted with a thorough dislike for the minister. The net result was one more stress added to those she already had.

Realizing too late the damage he had done to their relationship he tried without success to re-establish rapport with her over a period of many years. After each visit she would speak disparagingly about him to a neighbor. Never again did she attend his services of worship. Following that moment of displeasure in the minister, it is doubtful if he could reinstate an effective pastoral ministry. A pastor can seldom assist a person spiritually while the patient dislikes him.

Being Truthful

The pastor may be urged to convert a sick person whom he scarcely knows. Mrs. Y. called her pastor, saying, "Reverend, would you please call on Mr. X. who is very sick? He does not know the Lord and I am terribly worried about his soul. His wife is a good friend of mine. But, by all means don't tell him that I told you to call."

"Does Mr. X. have a church relationship?" the minister asked.

"No, he doesn't," she replied. "Mrs. X. belongs to a church but she could never get her husband to go with her."

"What should I tell Mr. X. when he asks me who told me to call on him?" the minister asked Mrs. Y.

"Maybe he won't ask you," she hedged.

"Since I have never called on him before he will most likely be interested in knowing how I happened to learn about him. Isn't that right?" the minister said.

She replied, "Could you say that a friend asked you to call without mentioning names?"

"I could," the minister responded, "but don't you think it would cause Mr. Y. to wonder why I will not tell him? Is there any reason why you do not want him to know that you are interested in his welfare?"

"Thinking about it like that," she said, "I suppose there really isn't any good reason why he shouldn't know that I called you. I just thought that maybe he wouldn't like my calling you."

"I assure you that I will not mention it to him unless he asks me," the minister said. "Thank you for calling."

The pastor is always at a disadvantage if he must hedge when the patient asks who sent him. The patient wonders why there must be secrecy. If he does not attend a church, as in the case of Mr. X., he immediately becomes suspicious of the pastor's intentions which builds a barrier of defensive behavior. In addition, when the minister does not extend his confidence to the patient by being truthful with him, the patient will respond in like manner.

When the patient suspects the reason for the minister's call and says so, the minister need not hesitate in being honest with him. In establishing rapport the pastor must extend his confidence to the patient.

Does Not Argue

In a similar situation, a pastor called upon an elderly lady, Mrs. A., after he introduced himself, she said, "I guess you think you're going to convert me, don't you?"

Rather shocked by the bluntness of her question, he was caught off guard and he said with a smile, "You won't mind if I try, will you?"

"You can try," she said, "but you won't succeed. Others have tried, too, and some of them were experts, let me tell you."

"So this has been going on for quite some time?" he smiled, responding to her mood.

"Indeed it has," she said. "Just about ever since I can remember. You can talk to me about a God of love all you want to but I won't believe a word of it. Ever since I was born God drew a circle around me. Inside the circle is unhappiness, outside of it is happiness. Every time I try to step into the other side, God slaps me in the face and knocks me back."

"So God has knocked you back into unhappiness a lot of times, you say?" he asked.

"When I was born I wasn't wanted. My parents shunted me on to relatives and when I grew up there wasn't a pretty thing about me. Look at me, be honest about it, can you see anything pretty about me? My hair's stringy, my eyes have no sparkle, my face never was pretty and now it's still worse with all the wrinkles. But even at that, I fooled them," she laughed. "I found a man and we were married. He was a good man, too. I did step outside the circle and I found happiness. But God couldn't stand to see me happy. He treated me dirty. My husband got killed in a railroad accident. I had joined his church, it was Episcopal, and the minister came and mouthed all kinds of nice things about God and I felt like saying, 'Oh, shut up. God hates me and you know it.' "

"You certainly have stated your case against God," the minister said. "If I am ever in trouble I certainly would like to have you on my side. Your side of the case certainly appears to have good reasons for thinking that God does not like you. Were you married very long before your husband died?"

"About four years," she said. "After that I got a job and worked for a number of years. I have enough money to keep me here in this apartment. I was getting along all right until this happened. I was going to invite a few friends and I went out to get some food. On the way back up the stairs, I stumbled, fell and broke my leg. That's why I have on this cast. You see, it's the same story. I was going to have a little happiness and He slapped me in the face again."

"Is there anything that I can do for you?" the minister asked.

"You mean around the apartment here?" she asked.

"Yes," he said.

"Now that's very kind of you," she said. "But, really there isn't. I can hobble around all right."

"I mean, are there any food supplies I can get for you, or anything like that?" he explained.

"The neighbor across the hall will help me," she said. "But I thank you just the same. Wouldn't it be something if I told the neighbors that a minister wanted to buy groceries for me!"

"I've done it on occasion for others," he said. "I don't see any reason why I should not do it for you if it would help you in any way."

"Well," she said. "You're about the nicest person I've ever met. And you haven't tried to convert me yet. Aren't you going to try?"

"Uh, uh," he said. "It's been a pleasure talking with you, and if you'll excuse me, I'll go on my way."

"I've enjoyed talking with you," she said. "If you have the time will you come back and visit with me again?"

"I appreciate your invitation," he said, smiling as he shook her extended hand. "The next time I can call as a friend and not as an intruder. I hope God will let you step over that line."

The minister conducted this call in splendid manner. He certainly established rapport with her whereas many who had previously called upon her had failed to do so. During the entire conversation he did not think that it was necessary to protect God's integrity, neither did he agree with her. She expected him to argue with her, but when he told her that she had stated her case very well and that he would like to have her as his lawyer, she knew that he respected her and sympathized with her. He seemed to perceive immediately that she had strong feelings of rejection and her story soon made it evident. When he kindly offered to help her in any way that he could, this raised him in her esteem for she appreciated kindness. In fact it caused her to remark that the neighbors would even be amazed that a minister would offer to buy groceries for her. Evidently she had not previously been treated too kindly by her minister. With her antagonistic attitude she could easily have frightened away any minister who might have wanted to help her. In this instance the minister communicated and Mrs. A. responded in her characteristically frank manner by saying that he was about the nicest person she had ever met. She invited him to return.

It would have been most disillusioning to Mrs. A. if the minister had not returned. But he did, and called upon her a number of times after that. Recall his statement that he hoped God would let her step over that line. In the ensuing months he succeeded in helping her understand her feelings of rejection and the reasons for them. Thereafter she achieved a measure of contentment she had not previously known.

Self-control, Understanding and Love

Important factors in establishing rapport are self-control, understanding and love. If the minister loses his self-control when he hears God maligned and thinks that he must immediately come to the defense of the Almighty he will, most likely, defeat his purpose. It must always be borne in mind that God's integrity and love are not annulled simply because the distraught person either doubts or denies them. God's existence is not precarious at all, neither are the emanations of His Being. The pastor can exercise patience in his pastoral relations with a person like Mrs. A. God will continue loving her whether she admits it or not. That is not the problem. The spiritual welfare of Mrs. A. is the pastor's first concern.

TWO

OUR SPIRITUAL DEFICITS

INTRODUCTION

It can be said that no person is perfectly adjusted in every emotional area of life. We can take minor emotional stresses in our stride without serious maladjustment. Most people can adjust to sickness without too intense emotional disturbances. For that reason the pastor will make many sick calls that are more or less routine. His presence is helpful in itself because he represents to the patient the concern of the church and our Lord. Even if his visit is comparatively brief and without prayer, it is helpful to the patient to know that his pastor was sufficiently interested to take the time to call. The pastor will use less of his time making calls of this nature than in counseling with fewer people who need his help in making adjustments or his guidance in arriving at decisions.

If the minister listens carefully to the patient, he can discern if the parishioner has spiritual or emotional problems which call for pastoral care. When the rapport is good, if the patient has a problem, he will lead the pastor to it either consciously or unconsciously. At the same time, the sensitive pastor will be alert in noticing indications of spiritual deficits.

Emotions or feelings of anxiety, fear, guilt, rejection, hostility, insecurity, jealousy, loneliness and despair may be regarded as spiritual deficits that are harmful in that they retard recovery and have a depressing effect upon the patient's mind. What is known about their harmful effects upon the body has been learned mainly through observation—a method used by psychologists. We can detect the effects of dishonesty by the "lie detector" which records the heart beat, the perspiration, and the respiration. That the emotions effect digestion is also well known. The exact degree to which the spiritual deficits retard recovery, however, has not been scientifically measured to the extent of recording the results accurately. Some progress has been made in the area, but the surface has hardly been scratched. It is now commonly accepted in medical science that somatic or physical disorders do bring about changes in the mind. It is also believed that mental attitudes may bring about organic changes. The exact degree of the interaction of these phases of personality has not yet been measured scientifically in all areas of behavior.

Fear

One of the most prevalent distresses in sickness is fear. It may vary on the emotional scale from intense fright to a mild fear anxiety. Since most people have been taught to believe that fear is cowardly, they are naturally reticent about expressing it unless it is very intense. Even under duress there are some who cannot bring themselves to admit that they are afraid. When a patient shows symptoms of extreme fear the surgeon may hesitate or postpone an operation. Sedatives may be administered by the physician the night before surgery to relax the patient.

The minister may open the way for the patient to express the reasons for his fears, if he has any, by remarking, "Many fine people whom I visit do express fear and in such situations I try to help them with it as much as I can."

With this statement the pastor has reassured the patient that fear is a normal reaction to a similar situation and nothing of which to be ashamed.

There are many reasons why a patient may be afraid, such as feelings of guilt, fear of pain, wondering if the operation or the disease may cause him or her to be physically impaired, or the fear of death itself.

Guilt

One of the most prevalent stresses that induce fear is a guilt anxiety. No one has always lived perfectly and when a person thinks

that he may face God suddenly any transgression may loom very large and important.

Helga was an unmarried lady in her seventies. She had lived an exemplary life but she had never joined the church. She did attend occasionally and gave liberally to the church through the pastor. She never wanted her name mentioned in connection with any good work that she did.

Helga became seriously sick and was taken to the hospital where it was found that she had an advanced case of cancer. The pastor called on her and found her very disturbed.

"I have cancer, Reverend," she said. "I am going to die and I am afraid."

"Helga," he said kindly, "you need not be afraid. God is good. He will take care of you. Think of all the fine things you have done. I know that you have never joined the church but you do more for the church than many wealthier members do. You need not be afraid. I'll read this psalm for you." He read Psalm 86 and prayed with her and left.

Two days later he called again and, when he asked her how she was, she replied, "So far I am fairly comfortable. The doctor is doing all that he can to keep me as comfortable as possible. It's only a matter of time, and I am still afraid."

"Helga, I had hoped you would not be afraid anymore," he said, trying to help her. "Always think of God as a God of love. He knows the good things you have done and He has redeemed you through Christ, our Saviour. God loves you, Helga."

After that reassurance he read to her the 121st Psalm and concluded the reading with prayer. Now, he hoped that he had definitely helped her.

Two days later he called upon her again. Her response to his greeting and question about how she was feeling was a disappointment to him because she said, "Your visits help me a lot but I am still afraid to die."

In sheer desperation he blurted out, "Helga, why in the world are you afraid of God?" It must have been the question she had hoped that he would ask. At long last he gave her an opportunity to tell him the reasons for her fears.

"I don't know if you know this," she started, "but I was raised a Catholic. Did you know that, Reverend?"

"No, I didn't," he said surprised, and relaxed in the chair to hear what more she had to say.

"I've never told this to anyone, Reverend," she said, "but now that I know I will soon die I do need some help."

"If I can help you, you know that I will," he said kindly. "What is it you want to tell me?"

"As I said," she started, "I was raised a Catholic and my parents were strict. I was confirmed in the church and everything was all right until I was a senior in high school. I fell in love with a boy and I thought that he loved me, too. It hurts me even to think about it. But I really loved him and one night in my home, my parents were asleep upstairs, I lost control of myself and had intercourse with him. I am so ashamed of it now, but I was sinful, very sinful, Reverend. And it has haunted me ever since."

"And this has worried you ever since," he repeated, thinking.

"After he had his way with me I was so ashamed that I never went with him again. I left my church rather than confess my sin to a priest. I never went with another boy and that is the reason I would not join your church. If I walked down that aisle to join the church I would hear God say, 'Helga, you sinner, what right have you to join a church? You're a hypocrite.'"

"So you have regretted this one rash act all of your life, Helga," he repeated. "Is that what you are telling me?"

"I was raised in a good home," she responded, "and I was a disgrace to my parents though they never knew it. What will God say to me?"

"Do you believe that God loves and is a forgiving God?" he asked seriously.

"I've tried to believe that," she responded.

"God has told us that if we repent and believe He is willing to forgive us. 'Though your sins be as scarlet, they shall be white as snow, though they be red like crimson, they shall be as wool' is the promise of our God," he assured her.

Because she knew that he was aware of the sin that had plagued her life, she could now accept his reassurance of God's forgiving

love. The next time that he called, Helga told him, "I am no longer afraid to die."

Fear and guilt often accompany each other, either one may precipitate the other.

Symptoms of Fear

In addition to verbal expressions of fear the observing pastor may notice symptoms of it such as bold statements, restlessness, talkativeness, disturbing dreams that may be told to him, and tears. When a sick person suddenly becomes very religious and wants religious literature and asks the pastor for helpful Scripture references to read, he may assume that the patient is troubled and be permissive. If good rapport exists and he permits the patient to talk with him, the causes of the religious tension will most likely be revealed. Once the patient can speak freely about the tension and/or the causes of it, the mind is usually receptive to reassurance which the pastor may offer through the Scripture and with prayer.

It is not always possible or may not even be advisable to try to convince a patient that fear of pain, for example, is unnecessary and should be avoided. We can also adjust to the presence of fear and use it creatively to be cautious, to take orders, and to follow the physician's advice. In addition, it may cause the patient to become more intimately related to God through the spiritual exercises of repentance, faith and courage. In this manner a spiritual deficit may be used for constructive purposes.

Rejection

Another prevalent spiritual deficit is the feeling of rejection which may precipitate hostility, loneliness, and despair.

An example of the feeling of rejection is Mrs. A. in Chapter I. Here the pastor succeeded in establishing rapport. He was helpful and she responded to his first visit in a friendly manner. The pastor was invited to return. Because he noticed that she appreciated his interest, he visited her a number of times. After the first visit he called her on the phone to determine a convenient time for visiting her in her apartment.

With each succeeding call she talked more freely about her life, her husband, the places where she spent her childhood and youth and where they lived after she was married. She explained that she was too old to have children, so she was deprived of that privilege also.

In addition, she became interested in the pastor and asked him about his life, his church, the congregation, his family and other personal interests. As he shared with her some of his concerns, she tried to help him with suggestions and ideas. This gave her a feeling of importance for she felt that she was helping him. During one of these visits, in her characteristically blunt manner, she asked, "Aren't you ever going to invite me to your church?"

"You told me that you are an Episcopalian," he responded, "and I don't want to be a sheep-stealer."

"What is a 'sheep-stealer'?" she asked.

"That is a minister who tries to win people away from their church to his church," he said.

She responded with a smile, "You know as well as I do that I haven't set foot in a church in years."

"That being the case," he said in her mood, "you may now consider yourself as being very officially invited." Then he added seriously, "I would be very pleased if you attended our church."

Mrs. A. did attend the church, joined the Golden Age organization where she found herself accepted and her talents appreciated. They formed a band and she became the drummer. Finally, in her seventies, she found the acceptance which she had desired so much throughout her life. With the happiness of acceptance and new interests, her feelings of hostility toward God slowly subsided.

Ego Injury

Every normal person wants to be accepted, to be loved and to feel important. The pastor will minister to many whose egos have been injured by real or fancied relationships that engender feelings of rejection.

Statements that may indicate rejection are: "Nobody cares if I live or die." "I can work myself to death around here and do you think anyone appreciates it?" "The only thing they're interested in down in this plant is the dollar sign. That's why I am where I am today." "I have to be on my deathbed to get any sympathy." "What have I done that God should punish me like this?" "No one cares about me enough even to visit me. Not one member of our church has called."

When any of these statements are made by a patient the pastor should take the time to listen to the details and attempt to help directly by examining with the patient his feelings of resentment. Through the conversation, compassion is shared and creative goals are visualized. The process often releases new energy and establishes hope.

The Man by the Pool

Human nature does not change through the years. Our Lord dealt with feelings of rejection also. The man by the pool (John 5: 1–15) was distressed with feelings of rejection that resulted in hostilities. Our Lord knew that this man's sickness was psychosomatic and had resulted in illness. Jesus asked him, "Do you want to be healed?"

The question clearly indicates that the man's illness was a matter of volition, that he was a hypochondriac nursing hostilities. This is evident in the man's reply, for he hedged, "Sir, I have no man to put me into the pool when the water is troubled, and while I am going, another steps down before me."

Other sick ones had a friend or a relative who cared enough to remain and help them. He felt that if his relatives or friends were more thoughtful of his welfare they would try to help him. In addition he resented it when others stepped down before him.

Our Lord was centuries ahead of His time in recognizing that this man was emotionally and spiritually ill. Through feelings of rejection he had retreated into hostility and despair. The despair is evident in the fact that he did not reply to Jesus' question in the affirmative and at the moment did not care if he ever recovered or not.

Our Lord also knew that a guilt complex in the first place must have started this chain reaction of spiritual deficits. Therefore, it was not enough just to heal this man physically. Further therapy was applied by Jesus when he purposely met the man later and said to him, "See you are well! Sin no more, that nothing worse befall you."

Directive Counseling

In this instance our Lord at first used directive counseling because He knew that the man was receptive to it and would be helped by it. Directive therapy must be used by a pastor very cautiously lest he intensify the stresses of the patient. In any event directive therapy can be helpful only to a limited degree.

Mrs. B. was a patient in a hospital. For three days her doctor tried to get her to go home but she preferred to remain in the hospital. Early in the morning of the third day there was an explosion on the floor beneath her room that caused the nurses to evacuate the patients immediately above and around the scene of the fire.

Later that morning her pastor visited Mrs. B. In the conversation she said, "You know, Reverend, early this morning we had a scare. The little nurse came in and said, 'Mrs. B., do you think you could walk out of this building?'

"And I said, 'Why no, my dear, I'm so weak I can hardly put my foot on the floor!' And she said, 'Well, all I'll say is you better try 'cause I think the buildin's on fire.'

"And you know what I did? I walked out of this buildin' and back in again. When the doctor comes this mornin' I think I'll tell him I'm agoin' home."

She went home that day carrying her problem with her, whatever it was. The directive therapy of the nurse did convince her that she should go home but it did not heal her illness. The pastor may think that with directive therapy he can be helpful to an ill person and at times it may seem that he is, but the parishioner is following the pastor's advice because he thinks that the minister will criticize or scold him if he does not. But this may soon become irksome because the problem is still there.

In the case of the man by the pool, John did not record in detail the conversation betwen Jesus and the man when our Lord approached him the second time. It is not revealed what sins caused the man's guilt complex, only the final statement which Jesus made. In what manner Jesus treated him will remain unknown because John could not record all that Jesus did, as he, himself, said. (John 20: 25.)

Loneliness

Feelings of rejection may also engender loneliness, one of the more personality-disorganizing spiritual deficits. There are many lonely sick people, especially among the aging. When anyone is sick for a considerable length of time, relatives and friends generally do lose interest and the patient becomes lonely.

The lonely patient craves attention and may go to any extreme to get it. Walter, aged about sixty, was sick for a long time recovering from excesses in drinking and carousing. His relatives paid little attention to him. His doctor ordered him to quit smoking, consequently the gray ladies could not bring him cigarettes. As a result Walter would call to anyone passing his room and beg a cigarette. He placed these under the sheet of his bed where he kept a supply of them.

After a while Walter became lonely. He felt that the nurses, the only ones who paid any attention to him, were neglecting him. One night there was brought into the second bed in his room a man who had evidently tried to cut his throat. Nurses, the doctor and orderlies worked feverishly to save the man's life and paid no attention to Walter.

Toward morning, when the attendants thought that the man was resting, they left the room one by one, until Walter was alone with the sleeping man. In a few moments that he was alone in the room, he broke a water glass on the floor and cut one of his wrists with a sliver of it. Thus he got the attention that he craved.

The Father of the New Baby

Sickness is often used by a lonely person to get the attention everyone craves. In childbirth the father may become sick in one manner or another and one can scarcely blame him for he receives precious little attention from anyone. The common explanation is that he is sick because of sympathy. Most likely, however, it is because he is lonely and subconsciously or consciously craves attention.

Realizing the father's dilemma in childbirth, most of our more modern hospitals today invite the husband to be with his wife in the labor and delivery rooms. His presence is supporting to his wife and he shares emotionally in the birth of their child.

In his ministry at the time of a birth, the pastor will be careful to give his attention to the father also. This ministry may be very helpful especially throughout the first months because the mother may center all her attention on the baby and neglect her husband. Most men can adjust quite well to the change but many cannot and do need spiritual help. If the mother notices that the pastor is also interested in the welfare of her husband, it may cause her to divert her attention from the baby at least enough to make him feel that he is still important in her life.

Critical of Others

Loneliness may also cause a patient or an aged person to become critical of others and the pastor will be cautious about believing everything that is told him by such a lonely patient.

One day the pastor called on Mr. C., an old man, who was taken to his married daughter's home because he was bedridden. The daughter remained in the room for a while and then left to go to a store a block away to make some purchases while the pastor was there.

As soon as Mr. C. knew that she was out of the house he said, "Reverend, I'm sorry to say that my daughter is a mean woman. She makes everybody believe that she takes care of me but she don't. She won't give me enough to eat and if I don't do what she wants me to do, she even beats me."

These remarks startled the pastor because he was of the opinion that the daughter was very kind and attentive to her father.

"I am surprised to hear you say that," the pastor remarked, "because I thought that she takes good care of you."

"That's it," the patient said. "Everybody thinks that, but I hain't had even my breakfast yet. What time o' day is it?"

The pastor looked at his wrist watch. "It is three o'clock," he said.

"There you have it," the old man said. "It's three o'clock and I hain't had a thing to eat yet. When Charley (his son-in-law) comes home she'll tell him how she fed me today."

Puzzled, the minister asked, "What do you live on if she doesn't give you any food?"

The old man ignored his question. Instead he slowly raised himself in the bed, stuck out his tongue and pointed to it. "Did you see that?" he asked.

"I saw your tongue," the minister said.

"Did you see the hole in it? She drove a nail through my tongue this morning," he said, lying back in the bed.

It was then that the pastor realized that the unfortunate old man was suffering with hallucinations, an ailment common to lonely old people.

"You are terribly mistaken about that, Mr. C.," the pastor argued, "your daughter has not driven a nail through your tongue."

"Hasn't she?" he asked, feeling momentarily relieved.

"Your daughter is good to you, Mr. C.," the pastor continued, "and I hope that you will believe me."

Old Mr. C. has so much time in which to do nothing that his imagination runs awry. This is commonly referred to as "hardening of the arteries" of the brain. The pastor may help the patient to temporary relief with directive counseling, but there is little chance for permanent help.

In these situations, when the loved one complains to the pastor that the patient does not appreciate anything that she does for him, the pastor may help her to understand that the sick one is not really responsible for his thoughts. Thus he may help her accept his apparent ingratitude. In instances such as this one, which are quite prevalent, the pastor will need to minister to members of the family of the patient also.

The lonely one may also become quite critical of the doctor: "He pays no attention to me. All he wants is my money," is a characteristic statement.

If the lonely patient is hospitalized, he may be critical of the hospital personnel, as well as the doctor. "Even the nurses don't pay any attention to me. I can ring and ring and ring and then maybe finally one of them will come in to see if I need anything."

The lonely one may be critical of the pastor. "Our minister never comes to see me, and when he does he acts like he can't wait until he can leave."

One elderly lady had a more subtle way of telling her pastor that he was not giving her enough attention. After he rang the door bell she let him wait a while. He knew that she was at home for this happened each time he called. He would ring again and she would slowly open the door, look at him and say, "Who are you?"

"I am your pastor," he would say. "Surely you know me."

"Oh, my goodness, it is," she would say. "It's been so long since you were here I didn't even know you any more."

She was a lonely old lady who craved attention.

Worry Over Children

A busy young mother may become lonely in a short while if she is a patient in a hospital. She thinks of her children and misses them. She will mention the children to her pastor and tell him that she is homesick for them.

The discerning pastor will not try to reassure her that they are getting along very well without her. Such support will, most likely, lead her to feel that she is not needed. She rightly feels that no one can care for her children quite as well as she can and she will want them to miss and need her.

Instead of this, the pastor will ask, "Who is caring for the children while you are here in the hospital?" He may be quite certain that her children are in the care of a responsible adult such as her mother or her mother-in-law. He will be helpful if he permits her to talk about the children and express her concern for their welfare.

She may say very little about her husband because he calls upon her every day or because she knows that he is capable of providing for his own needs.

If the pastor is acquainted with the one who has custody of the children, after the patient has had an opportunity to express herself, he may assure her that they will get along as best they can until she is home again to care for them. This support confirms her desire to be needed and missed at home. At the same time she has had the relief of expressing any anxiety she might have about their welfare.

When the mother expresses real concern about the children, he may offer to visit them to ascertain if her concerns are real or fancied. This may seem to be a needless waste of his time and effort, especially if the children are in the custody of a responsible adult. However, by offering to visit them, he lets the mother know that he is interested in their wellbeing. The children will appreciate his call and the one who is caring for them will know that he is interested in them.

Only on very rare occasions will he find that the children are being neglected. If he finds that to be the situation he may call upon the father and consult with him about it. It is advisable for him to wait until the situation has been corrected before he visits the mother again in order to be truthful in assuring her that her children are getting as good care as anyone other than their mother can give them. However, it should be emphasized that only on rare occasions will the pastor find children of his parish being neglected while their mother is sick in a hospital.

The Husband of a Sick Wife

In this connection it should be mentioned that on some occasions the husband of a sick wife who is away from home may resort to excessive drinking. The wife may tell her pastor that her husband is drinking too much. If he is not an alcoholic, the pastor may be helpful to him by calling upon him. This does happen occasionally and poses a serious problem.

Despair

Another spiritual deficit that disturbs many sick people is despair. The will to live is very important in any patient's recovery. Today I overheard a surgeon in conversation with the husband of a young woman who had been so seriously sick that the surgeon and all of us thought she would not recover. Her blood pressure suddenly sank after surgery. The surgeon, an internist and nurses worked frantically to save her life with intravenouses, medications and every available medical resource. The husband said, "Doctor, I don't know how I can ever thank you, you saved her life."

"It was more than that," I heard the surgeon say to him.

The husband paused, waiting.

"It was her will to live and the blessing of God," he said, as he looked at the chart in his hand.

Incentives to live are important motivations in the process of recovery from any serious sickness. When the patient does not care if he recovers or not or when he looks forward to death as a release from misery or loneliness, the healing processes are definitely retarded.

The pastoral ministry to the patient in despair who does not want to recover will be conditioned by the sick one's philosophy of life and death. If the patient regards health as being desirable only if it can be used for constructive purposes, the pastor may help the patient in despair to perceive constructive purposes for living.

It must always be borne in mind that death is not final for the Christian, nor should it be regarded as defeat. It is the business of physicians and nurses to keep people alive in this world as long as they can and, for them, death always means failure of their purposes. The pastor's objectives or purposes reach beyond any span of years a person might live in this world and from the spiritual point of view death is not at all final.

The patient in despair does not always want to die. In most instances the despair is occasioned by a lack of incentives to live but the patient does hope that some day things will be different. When any adverse situation is regarded as final the patient may become very depressed. We can tolerate almost any unpleasant sensations or pressures as long as we know that they are temporary. It is when the patient cannot see a way out of the unpleasant situation or the possibility of release that despair becomes a problem.

Factors in Despair

Among the precipitating factors of despair are prolonged pain, lack of incentives to live and intense feelings of rejection. The pastoral approach in situations of despair will depend upon the various factors that may be involved. If the patient is old and weary and expresses the desire to die, it is not helpful to the patient to argue that he should want to live longer in this world. From the Christian point of view death is not final. The pastor may well permit the aged one to express hopes for release from the burden of the flesh and anticipations in regard to the eternal life.

However, when the patient is needed in the home, the church, or society, the pastor may be helpful in guiding the thoughts in that direction. It may require much patience and ability to assist the sick one into accepting objectives for constructive living.

Family Situations

Family situations may cause feelings of despair. A young husband and father, about 38 years old, just did not care if he recovered or not. The reasons for his despair were the extravagance of his wife, her slovenly housekeeping and her lack of response to his sexual needs. "No matter how much I would earn, we'd still be head over heels in debt. Our house always looks like a hog pen and the only time I get any relief is when I almost have to fight for it. There's just no use going on living. I'm tired of it all."

This young couple needs the assistance of a family counseling center and the pastor will be helpful to both of them if he can lead them to see this need and the possibility of bettering their situation.

Suicidal Tendencies

When the patient feels so intensely rejected that he talks about suicide, the pastor should counsel the patient to receive psychiatric treatment. The prevalent opinion that people who threaten suicide never commit it is fallacious. When a patient is so deeply in despair that he contemplates taking his own life, the pastor definitely ought to call this to the attention of the physician and consult with him about it.

Religious Doubt

Religious doubt is another spiritual deficit that may develop in any serious sickness. Precipitating factors may be the length of sickness, the cost of the treatment, the prognosis of the disease, and the patient's concepts of God. The latter factor is probably the one that precipitates the religious doubt more so than the others. The person who regards the Almighty as a Benevolent Force who bestows only blessings upon His children and protects them from any calamity because of their faithfulness is susceptible to religious doubts when such favors are not forthcoming.

Mr. D., about 45 years old, a skilled laborer, sang in the choir of the church and belonged to the men's Brotherhood as well. He was faithful in his religious duties, and his wife was also interested in the church and sang in the choir.

Mr. D. was involved in an auto accident that badly mangled his right leg. For about three months the orthopedic surgeon tried to save the leg but it would not heal. It was then decided that to save his life the leg would have to be amputated.

During his long sickness his pastor was faithful in visiting him. At the conclusion of each call the minister would say, "Shall we have a word of prayer, together?" Taking for granted that Mr. D. found some comfort in prayer, his pastor scarcely waited for an affirmative reply.

The first time the pastor noticed a change in Mr. D.'s attitude was in the third month of his sickness. When he asked the usual question, Mr. D. was quick to reply, "You can if you want to."

The minister was puzzled with this reply and the next time he called he gave Mr. D. opportune time to answer his question.

Mr. D. said, "You can if you want to."

Since they had known each other for a long time, his pastor

said, "Your answer puzzles me. Would you rather that I do not pray with you?"

"Since you ask me, Reverend," Mr. D. replied, "it doesn't make any difference if you do or if you don't."

"Do you mean that prayer doesn't make any difference to you?" the pastor asked.

"I might as well be honest with you," the patient explained. "I've had plenty of time to think. I've come to the conclusion that if there is a God He certainly does not pay much attention to the people who try to do the right things."

"You feel that God has let you down?" the minister asked.

Mr. D. knew that the minister understood what he meant and he was in a mood to talk about it.

"Frankly, I've about come to the conclusion that there is no God at all. If there is, He is mighty cruel and I don't care to have anything to do with Him. The doctors are now talking about amputating my leg. Think of what that is going to do to me."

"Would you care to tell me what you think that it will do to you, if it comes to that?" the minister asked.

"In the first place I'm going to be laid up for a long time," he started. "Compensation and insurance will take care of a lot of the expense. But my wife has to live, too. The two boys are old enough to take care of themselves, but I had hoped to send the young one to college. Now, that can't be."

"You are sure the boy won't get to college," the pastor remarked.

"I doubt if I will be able to do my job with one leg," he continued, "if I have a job left when and if I ever get back to it. And I've been thinking, too, I wonder how my wife is going to take it . . . with me hobbling around the place and going to bed with only one leg.

"I've tried to live a Christian life . . . as much, I think, as at least the average Christian and we've worked in the church through these years and as thanks for it, God, if there is one, let this happen to me. I don't want to be ugly to you, Reverend. I respect you, you know that. But I'll be honest with you, I've actually cussed God and would rather He would let me be."

"Would you rather, then, that I do not call on you anymore?" the minister asked.

"I wouldn't say that," the man answered. "I like you as a friend. When you have time, I'll be glad to see you."

The pastor took a chance when he asked Mr. D. if he would rather that he did not call in the future. The patient might have replied in the affirmative and thus closed the door to any further help from his pastor.

Mr. D. expressed thoughts that often plague a person who has enjoyed good health and is suddenly incapacitated for a long period of time. The patient may turn his resentment toward God, more so if his philosophy of faith is that God should prosper and protect those who try to be faithful to Him. When God fails to do this, the patient's faith will have to be readjusted and in the process of rethinking his relationship to God, it is quite normal to follow the path of least resistance and deny God's existence. By doing this the patient does not have to contend with readjusting his beliefs. At the same time, however, one who has previously been quite content with his faith may become quite bitter in his outlook on life, as Mr. D. has done.

The pastor must place himself in Mr. D.'s position and in the ensuing calls try to help him to more hopeful anticipations of the future. With his visits the pastor will communicate to Mr. D. that God has not forsaken him entirely. After the amputation, the pastor may encourage him by helping him realize that he will not be incapacitated indefinitely. Mrs. D. can be helpful in this situation if she can let him know that he will not be less attractive to her. This problem, however, will not be resolved in his mind until after he has returned to his home. It is one of his worries for he alluded to it when he said, "and going to bed with only one leg." The pastor may be helpful to him through counseling with Mrs. D. before he returns to their home.

It is essential that the pastor maintains a friendly relationship with Mr. D. throughout the process of recuperation. Since he has invited the minister to continue to call upon him he has not identified the pastor with God in his religious doubts. As a Roman Catholic may identify God with his church and the Jew his synogogue, many Protestants link the minister very closely with God. As a result of this identification, when faith in God is shattered, the patient may also become indifferent or even antagonistic toward the minister whom he regards as being on God's side in any situation.

Mr. D.'s faith in God was based upon a false assumption that the Almighty always favors with physical protection those who serve Him. In the ancient history of God's chosen people, the Almighty did use this method to educate primitive minds. Serve God and prosper, neglect God and suffer was the prevalent ideology of the Old Testament, until man developed sufficient spiritual strength to accept the concepts of the Book of Job. God's revelation of His holy will is progressive in the Scripture but, unfortunately, some Christians cannot make the leap of faith past the border of despair.

As Mr. D. adjusts emotionally and mentally to his physical handicap, the pastor can help him accept his condition with determination to make the best possible use of it. He may be encouraged to seek the aid of a professional vocational guidance counselor who may indicate to him the specific areas of endeavor for which he has the average or more than average ability.

Sexual Relations

In the area of his sexual relations with his wife, since Mr. D. mentioned it as one of his problems, his pastor may listen to him carefully as he is recuperating. However, Mr. D. will find that he is no less attractive to her if he can adjust in other areas and maintain his dignity. If she loves him, she will help him so that he will be in a position to express his love for her in the sexual embrace in other than the usual accepted method of the male role, should that be necessary.

Other Factors in Religious Doubt

As he adjusts in the various areas of living, in all probability his resentment toward God will vanish. The pastor will find that many people whose faith has been shattered or shaken by any misfortune do emerge from the situation spiritually stronger than they were previously, if they were at one time faithful as Mr. D. was. In every such situation the pastor will need to exercise the patience that comes

from understanding. He will not be helpful by arguing with the ill one to defend God or by leaving the impression that the patient is a sinner for doubting God's love or His existence.

When the cost of the treatment exceeds the patient's financial ability, or the prognosis indicates that major changes in his life can be expected, possibly incapacitation over a long period of time; these factors may induce religious doubts. The ill one may feel that God has forsaken him, and such spiritual stress may also be accompanied by feelings of despair.

THREE

OUR SPIRITUAL RESOURCES

INTRODUCTION

In his ministry to the sick the pastor will visit mostly the members of his congregation and those who attend and support his church as non-member adherents. However, in addition to these he may be called upon to minister to others who have no church relationship, as well as some who have not transferred their membership to the church in the community where they are living.

Basic Religious Beliefs

To avoid being judgmental it should be said that in most instances of sincere skepticism there are factors that engender it in the life of an individual. Mrs. A. in Chapter I was undoubtedly regarded as a skeptic by those who knew her as well as by the pastors who had previously called upon her. In reality she was a woman who sincerely desired guidance out of her feelings of antagonism toward God. In Chapter II, Mr. D. needed help in modifying his original religious concepts which proved inadequate for his adjustment to his physical disability. He had sufficient basic religious beliefs with which eventually to affect a satisfactory readjustment.

It can be said that almost everyone in America has religious beliefs of varying degrees and nature. Through T.V., radio, the public press, the movies and conversations, even people who never attend any church are exposed to religious ideas. Even the "wino" who spends his hazy awake hours begging enough money to buy another bottle of oblivion does pass churches, church bulletin boards and has a piece of newspaper to read.

I have tried to minister to a few of them in the hospital. Most of them never experience the luxury of dying in a hospital with, at the least, some nurses around to care. One of them, in his semiconscious delirium, would raise his hand with an imaginary bottle in it and move his mouth as if in the act of drinking from it.

In his brief moments of semi-lucidness I tried to tell him that I was a "preacher." It must have penetrated his mental haze and meant something to him, for once he muttered, "Pray for me." The only other words any of us heard him say were, "Oh, God." Ordinarily one would think that such a derelict never gave God a thought. I spoke to him the Twenty-Third Psalm and Tenth Chapter of John. There was no response other than a very faint smile which led me to believe that at times he heard what was said. I tried to reassure him of God's love before he breathed his last breath. After a prayer commending his soul to God, the two nurses who were at his bedside and I gave vent to our feelings of pity with sincere tears.

Trivia That Induce Stress

This incident is mentioned to illustrate that almost everyone with whom the pastor will come into contact will have some religious beliefs, even people who have never attended a church. In other instances it may be more difficult for a pastor to minister to a person whose religious concepts have been warped or twisted by self-appointed and uneducated "preachers" who make eternal salvation dependent upon a "holiness" that no human can achieve or should even want to attain. God could not possibly be so cruel as to condemn for eternity a person guilty of some of the trivia that some religious bigots insist are important.

I mention this because such trivia may become major religious problems with seriously sick people who have violated tenets they have been indoctrinated to believe essential to eternal salvation. Recently I counseled with a woman who was intensely disturbed because she believed that she had succumbed to temptation by wearing lipstick.

These people are usually very conscientious and sincere and the pastor will need to understand their misgivings about violating trivial sectarian taboos. He may help them find the sense of forgiveness through sincere repentance or guide them into more wholesome conceptions of God's love.

The Three Primary Resources

Our three primary spiritual resources are faith, hope and love which the Apostle Paul discussed in I Corinthians 13. Paul's theology was based upon the teachings of Jesus revealed to him through the Holy Spirit and the Apostles who had associated with our Lord personally. Thus the apostle emphasized the importance of these Christian virtues in healthful living.

Faith

It should be mentioned, however, that our Lord healed some who gave no evidence of faith in Him at the time that the healing occurred. The paralytic at Bethzatha (John 5: 1–15) and the man blind from birth (John 9) are examples of this. In both instances through the healing process the sick ones were guided into faith. It should also be noted that Jesus was interested in more than the healing of a disease. Other purposes were also accomplished in His healing miracles.

On other occasions Jesus definitely emphasized the therapeutic powers of faith in the healing of the centurion's slave (Luke 7: 1–10) and the woman who suffered twelve years with an issue of blood. (Luke 8: 42–48) We may conclude from these examples that in certain instances of healing our Lord considered faith as an important element. In others, He used the healing to engender faith. In all four of them He considered faith in Him important to the individual as a way of life.

While faith in God does have healing qualities, a patient without much faith in God may be cured of a disease. This does not necessarily indicate that the cured person is well and healthy because he is not physically sick. On the contrary, a physically well person may be spiritually ill and be not aware of it until it affects him physically or mentally.

Faith is an inclusive term and may be interpreted to mean con-

fidence in the physician, the capability of the nurses and the healing
potentials of the surgery or the medication. It is generally accepted
that when a sick person loses confidence in these healing media,
his recovery may be retarded. We know that feelings of antagonism
or insecurity affect the functioning of the endocrine glands but we
do not know exactly why and how this happens.

Faith may also be construed to mean confidence in self or in the
ability of the body to recover from sickness. "I know I'll get over
this. I've gone through other things before and managed to survive,"
is typical of this confidence. "You can get a good man down but you
can't keep him there," is another example of confidence in the healing forces of the body. Such "faith" may have therapeutic influence
regardless of those who ridicule or depreciate the values of "positive
thinking." Christian Science, New Thought, Unity and other move-
ments emphasize the importance of this type of positive thinking and
many people are helped by them.

Therapeutic Values of Faith

We can include this philosophy in our pastoral work although
by "faith" we mean confidence in God's love and care, and especially
the revelation of it in Jesus Christ and His redeeming grace. This is
the faith that is one of our primary spiritual resources.

This faith in God does various things for us. In the first place it
helps us to think on a level with God's thoughts as far as that is possible for us with our limited mental and spiritual acuity. With faith
we do not make impossible demands upon God but rely upon His
wisdom and love.

Through faith in Him we know that there is more to life than
physical health, although it is very important while we are living in
this world. At the same time we also know that the physical body is
mortal but the soul is eternal. If it should be for the benefit of the
soul God will grant physical healing either through the ministration
of physicians and medication or through divine intervention or both.
Speaking with the daughter of a male patient who was sent home to
die of cancer more than a year previously, she said, "My father is
getting along fine. It is truly a miracle. God has answered our prayers

and we can never thank Him enough or the physician who helped all that he could." Through faith we have confidence in God's love and care for us.

Faith in God enables us to accept sickness or calamity without the additional spiritual burdens of hostility, rebellion or despair. A lady in her sixties lay helplessly shaking with palsy. Her pastor expected her to complain about her condition, but to his surprise she said, "I rely upon God who through prayer gives me the strength to live from day to day until He sees fit to call me home."

The pastor may help the patient use whatever resources of faith he may have to meet his specific problem. Faith may serve to alleviate feelings of rejection, loneliness and antagonism toward God.

Hope

Hope grows naturally out of faith in God. Even a toothache is unbearable as long as there is no hope for relief. So, the patient may have hope for better days that are coming. For the Christian there is always a tomorrow and the hope that the sun will dispel the clouds. Even when the disease is terminal and the patient is aware of it, the pastor can sustain his hope for a brighter tomorrow. (I Corinthians 15: 19, Revelations 21: 1–4)

Our faith in God provides the assurance that He cares. Whatever occurs to us in relation to sickness will eventually run its course, and God's plan for us is good and purposeful. We may use it for our spiritual benefit while it is happening and plan for the future with the deeper insight gained from the experience.

Faith and hope are mingled in the following situation. Both the patient and the pastor, through the guidance of the Holy Spirit, used the situation for their benefit.

Mrs. E. was a kindly, white-haired widow of 70. Quite active, she devoted much of her time to the church. "If you need me for anything," she told her pastor, "and I can do it, you call me. I have plenty of time to help in the church wherever I can, whenever you need me." Mrs. E. lived alone although she had a married daughter living in the same community.

The incident happened one winter Sunday night. Mrs. E.

served refreshments to the youth group that met in the church. The clouds spread a thin spray of rain that froze on the sidewalk. As Mrs. E. was leaving the church, she slipped on the steps and fractured her pelvis. She insisted upon going to her home, and the doctor who was called brought a stretcher. With the aid of some of the youths she was carried to her home a few blocks from the church. Her daughter was summoned and came to help care for her. After she was as comfortable as they could make her, the young minister prayed with her and went to his home.

He could not sleep. He was angry with God and spent most of the night arguing with the Almighty. If this had to happen why did God pick on Mrs. E.? Why did He not let it happen to someone who was less faithful to Him? How could he teach the young people that God is a God of love when He lets something like that happen to a faithful soul like her? And why, oh why, of all places, did it have to happen on the church steps? Any place other than the church steps would have been bad enough. Can't God even protect His faithful servants in His own house?

With such disturbing thoughts he was too angry to pray for understanding.

The next morning he decided to call on Mrs. E. because he had been taught in the seminary that it was a minister's duty to call upon the sick. He hedged as long as he could and finally went. It was raining . . . a dreary day! "You could at least let the sun shine," he said angrily to God as he walked in the rain. "What must she think of You! And I agree with her. If I could think of anything else to do I'd get out of the ministry."

He was in this frame of mind as the daughter admitted him to the home and told him that her mother had eaten breakfast. When he walked into the room, she smiled to him and said, "It's such a bad day outside I didn't expect you to come."

"I hope you are resting fairly well," he said.

"Much better than I thought that I would," she responded with a smile, "and I thank the Lord for that."

He breathed a sigh of relief because, if she had said, "I think God has let me down," he would most likely have responded, "I agree with you. I think that He has let us both down."

She continued, "I doubt if I can take care of the refreshments for the youth meetings for a while so I told my daughter to ask Mrs. _____ if she will do that now. She may enjoy it and when I am well again she may want me to help her. I was getting so selfish, Reverend, that I thought I had to do it all by myself. Other people want God to use them, too."

Fortunately, the young minister was sufficiently wise to hold his tongue and listen to her. During the ensuing calls he learned that she did not regard her accident as having been permitted by God or visited upon her or that He had mistreated her. "I should have been more careful," she said on one occasion. "At my age I'm not as spry as I used to be."

On another occasion she shared with him that she never really knew the meaning of patience until this happened to her. She spoke with him about her plans for her future activities in the church when she could walk again. She spoke of her husband's kindness and her hopes of being with him in heaven. In addition she found joy in the expressions of friendship and love extended to her by people of the church and others.

As in many counseling situations, this pastor was helped by the patient through her expressions of faith and hope and love. At the same time he supported her more than he thought by listening to her and learning how a seasoned Christian may use spiritual resources to maintain spiritual and emotional equilibrium during a crisis.

Love

Love is the third spiritual resource mentioned by Paul in the triangle of Christian virtues. Love, like faith, is a general term with many specific connotations, each of which is healthful. In general the term signifies a spiritual attitude which carries over into various relationships: love for God, for our fellowman, more specifically toward our friends, relatives and neighbors. More difficult of achievement is an attitude of love toward those who do not like us. (Matthew 5: 44, Luke 6: 27, 35)

As a spiritual resource love has healing qualities in its many phases. The love of God helps us overcome feelings of being rejected by Him and inspires us to look beyond ourselves for fulfillment in service to Him. The same principle applies in our attitude toward others. The Good Samaritan found freedom of expression in it. (Luke 10: 30–37) Through love for his fellowman the Good Samaritan could ignore prejudices and express his concern for the welfare of the wounded man by the side of the road. At the same time selfish interests did not enter his thoughts. He saw a man in need and love motivated him to do what he could to help him.

As expressed toward our friends, relatives and neighbors it helps us handle constructively any offenses that might otherwise result in hostilities, feelings of revenge or hatred, all of which are spiritually unhealthy. Love also helps the patient overcome negative thoughts of being neglected and fosters a wholesome relationship of gratitude and fellowship.

Should any who are near the patient in the roles of relatives or friends, by acts of neglect or anger give cause for being offended, through Christian love these offenses can be overlooked or forgiven.

God's love for us is expressed in the atonement and our redemption. "Jesus forgave even His enemies who crucified Him," a woman patient said, "Surely I should forgive people who offend me. It is a good spiritual exercise for me."

As Christ died for us we no longer live for ourselves but for Him . . . to reflect His love that is in our hearts.

Sense of Joy

In addition to faith, hope and love we have other resources for healthful spiritual living, however, all of them emanate to a degree from these three fundamental ones. There is, for example, the Christian's sense of joy. If there are any groups of people who have reasons to rejoice, certainly Christians should be among them. Through our faith we can appropriate the spiritual benefits of our Lord: forgiveness, life and salvation both temporal and eternal. With these blessings we can have a sense of joy.

Our knowledge of human nature and our experience of God's love help us to rejoice even in trying situations. With them we can face reality without being unduly disturbed spiritually. In addition they aid us in adjusting to personal injuries.

A pastor was stopped on the street by a man whom he knew only by sight who said to him, "I want to apologize to you for the way I acted when you called on my friend the other afternoon."

"You will have to jog my memory," the pastor said, "because I do not know for what you are apologizing."

"I was visiting my sick friend when you came in the room," the man said.

"Yes, I recall that," the pastor answered.

"And I did not speak to you," the man said. "I don't know why I did that except that for the moment I resented your coming in and I apologize for it."

"Please don't give it another thought," the pastor said. "I noticed that you did not speak to me but I figured that there was a reason for it. There are times when I feel that way also."

Realizing the forgiveness of God in his own life gave this minister a sense of joy. It enabled him to accept this man's intended slight without rancor.

A sense of joy may also be achieved through Holy Communion. In the observance of it one may experience God's forgiveness and an attitude of charity toward others.

In many Protestant Churches, Holy Communion is observed as a sign of our Lord's perpetual love and of His redeeming grace. Pastors of these denominations offer this sacrament to the sick, especially at those seasons of the year when Holy Communion is observed in the Church. By offering to administer the sacrament to the sick on such occasions it will not be regarded as a last rite but rather as communion with the Lord in fellowship with all believers.

Repentance

Repentance is a progressive experience consisting of acknowledgment of sin, sorrow or regret over sin, confession of it to God, a determined purpose not to engage in the disturbing sin again and a longing for God's grace. This spiritual exercise should result in a conviction that God accepts the sincere repentance and offers forgiveness.

However, for some people the general confession of sin does not meet the specific need of the one who is seeking forgiveness. A patient expressed it to her pastor in this way, "I feel that this confession is not deep enough." When he paused in the ritual of communion and asked if she desired to make her confession more personal, she did so, mentioning a particular transgression which was troubling her.

In such instances the pastor will be helpful if he can assist the patient through the progressive stages of repentance until the confession does meet his or her spiritual needs. Once that has been achieved, the pastor may reassure the patient's conviction of forgiveness with words of absolution.

It must be borne in mind that repentance and confession are the catharsis that produce the healthful sense of being forgiven. Ministers are usually very kind people and are therefore prone to offer reassurance of forgiveness prematurely. This may cause the sick one to believe that the pastor does not understand the need or takes it too lightly.

Absolution

On the other hand, the minister should be careful not to withhold the reassurance of forgiveness when the sick one has expressed sincere repentance and longs for God's grace. A sense of being forgiven by God will help the patient extend the same grace to others. (Matthew 18: 23–35) It also increases his experience of joy.

All of these spiritual resources have their origin or are related to the three primary healing virtues: faith, hope and love. In addition, patience, courage and gratitude also emanate from them. The latter three resources will be discussed more adequately in Part II.

In summary, it may be said that the foregoing are the more important spiritual resources available to the people to whom the pastor ministers. Each one will have some of these resources in varying degrees. The pastor will help his people use these resources to meet any spiritual deficits that may trouble them.

THE PASTOR'S RELATION TO THE DOCTOR

From the dawn of recorded history the more discerning people have somehow realized that religion and healing are interrelated. Through the centuries medicine was developed into a science but religion is not a science. Perhaps it is for man's benefit that the two parted ways for a time in Western civilization.

The Total Personality

Our blessed Lord was centuries in advance of His age when He used divine forces in the healing of physical ailments. He realized that man is a total personality that cannot be divided three ways into body, mind and soul. We are beginning to realize that health and wholeness involves all three phases of man's being. Lest we become too secure in our self-confidence it may be said that most likely there are phases of man's health and wholeness of which we are totally unaware. How Jesus raised Lazarus from the dead is as much a mystery today as it was when He first performed the miracle. We express our lack of understanding with the word "miracle."

As medicine and surgery developed into a science, the selfishness inherent in human nature caused learned men in the field of medicine to look askance at religionists. In many instances the clergy gave them good reasons for their attitude and some of them still do.

Religious Taboos

The physician has seen so many taboos promoted by the clergy—the taboo against birth control or the administration of a blood transfusion or an intravenous injection or a vaccine are examples—and attempts by the clergy to regulate the practice of medicine, that it is understandable that some physicians regard the clergy with suspicion.

Much of the distrust on the part of physicians has been dispelled, but much still justifiably remains. In this book we cannot present the details of the movement toward a better understanding between medicine and religion that has developed in our century. Most significant in this area of understanding was the publication in 1936 of *The Art of Ministering to the Sick* by Russell L. Dicks and Richard Cabot.

We have come a long way since that time and we are only at the beginning. What will develop in the future will be determined in the main by the learning, devotion and the attitude of the clergy.

The Skilled Clergyman

Today, the doctor expects the clergyman to have a commensurate measure of professional skill. He does not want the pastor to diagnose the disease and/or suggest the kind of medical and surgical treatment that is needed. He knows that at times he must use the facilities of modern medical laboratories to determine the nature of the disease and the treatment that might cure it. He resents it when the minister observes the patient and diagnoses the ailment. The doctor rightfully regards this as amateurish and harmful to the one who is sick.

The doctor has spent many years preparing himself for his profession. In addition, he spends much time and effort in additional training each year. He expects the minister to be just as adequately prepared to exercise his pastoral office. He has no respect for an uneducated and inadequately prepared pastor and may not even tolerate the ministry of such a clergyman to his patient.

If he finds his patient disturbed by the pastor's call, he may ask that the minister not be permitted to visit and communicate the reasons for it to the patient or to members of the family. When the minister calls thereafter a member of the family may tell him that the patient is too sick to see him or cannot have visitors.

The doctor regards every person who is called "Reverend" as a minister. He does not have time to make distinctions. Generally, he knows only the requirements for ordination in his own church and that of the Roman Catholic clergy. He may become hostile when he finds that the minister who is calling upon his patient has little or no preparation for the tremendously important work of a pastoral ministry to the sick. He does not want his patient plagued with threatening "religious" literature such as, "What If You Should Die at Midnight?" or "What Hell Is Like," or "Where Will I Spend Eternity?"

Mutual Respect and Confidence

The physician expects the clergyman to discern when the patient has spiritual problems without the necessity of calling it to the pastor's attention. Generally, the doctor will not try to heal spiritual tension because he considers himself to be inadequately trained in that area.

In most situations the doctor will be grateful if the minister can support the patient's confidence in his ability to treat the sickness because he knows that confidence in the physician is important in the healing process. In this respect it is advantageous for the minister to know the physician personally. In the same vein the doctor may want to support the patient's respect for the minister when there is mutual respect and confidence.

The minister will want to keep open avenues of approach to the physician by personal contact either by phone or by calling at his office. The physician may be able to help him in his ministry to the patient. This is of special significance when the patient's family relies upon the counsel of the pastor regarding the future treatment of the patient. The minister may need to know the doctor's opinion regarding the length of the convalescence or the chances for recovery or how helpless the patient may become. Many physical factors of the sickness may influence the pastor in his ministry not only to the patient but to members of the family. The doctor will appreciate the clergyman's cooperation for the future welfare of his patient.

When the pastor thinks that he can more adequately minister to the needs of a parishioner through more information about the nature of the disease and the prognosis, he may contact the physician and state his concern. The doctor may discuss with him specific problems of the patient and the spiritual therapy that he thinks is needed. If the physician hesitates to confide, the pastor may explain how important the diagnosis and prognosis is to his pastoral work.

An instance of a violation of this mutual confidence was a case in which the doctor told the minister that the middle-aged woman patient was suffering from hysteria. There was no indication of any organic reason for her lameness. "Her difficulty, I am sure, is mental,

Reverend," the doctor said to him. "I believe you can help her more than I can."

In this instance, unfortunately, the minister somehow conveyed to her what the doctor had told him. Her response was, "Are you trying to tell me that that doctor thinks I'm crazy?" That doctor will not confide in a clergyman again for a long time. Fortunately such incidents of violation of confidence are rare on the part of both clergy and physicians.

However, when the patient confesses to the clergyman confidential matters, these must not be shared with the doctor or any other person. If the pastor thinks that the information may help the physician in treating the patient he may ask the patient if he may share it with the doctor and explain his reasons for asking.

The minister expects the doctor to respect his intelligence and skill, for many clergymen have spent an equal number of years preparing themselves for their vocation and attend many seminars and workshops to keep abreast of the developments in their field of service.

THE CLERGYMAN AND THE NURSE

The nurse may be very helpful to the pastor in his ministry to the patient. Her attitude toward him will, however, depend upon her training and the previous experiences she has had with clergymen. If the nurse has been educated in a church-related school of nursing, she has most likely been conditioned to receive the clergyman as one who should be given preference in visiting the sick. In some of these schools of nursing courses are offered in religious philosophy and these nurses may regard the minister as one of the healing team.

The Patient's Chart

The pastor is not permitted to read the patient's chart or make notations upon it. This record is regarded as confidential and may be read only by the attending physician. The chart may be used as evidence in a law suit but only when subpoenaed by a court order. Embarrassment to nurse and pastor can be avoided if the clergyman refrains from asking to read the patient's chart.

The fact that the minister is not permitted to read the patient's chart or record anything of significance in it, may indicate that he is not accepted by the medical authorities as a vital segment of the therapeutic team. If in the nurse's opinion, something of significance has happened with the patient as a result of the pastoral visit she may write it into the chart. If the minister wishes to leave a note for the attending physician she will slip it into the chart so the doctor will read it.

The Minister's Approach

If the minister is unknown to the nurses on a nursing unit of a hospital he will receive better cooperation if he introduces himself to the head nurse before making his call. This courtesy is especially important if he is calling during non-visiting hours. Generally, ministers are permitted or encouraged (depending on hospital policy) to call upon their patients at any time. When the minister should call will be discussed in Part II, Chapter IV. It is understandable that a nurse may object to an unidentified man calling upon a patient at other than visiting hours, more so, if the doctor has ordered no visitors for the patient. To avoid any misunderstanding the pastor should place his card in front of the nurse, introduce himself, and inform her whom he intends to visit. This introduction also makes it possible for the nurse to impart to him any significant emotional or spiritual manifestations of the patient that the nurses have observed.

The private duty nurse may not leave the room while the pastor is calling. She has been taught to remain in the room while the doctor is treating the patient and may think that the pastor wants her to stay. If he wishes to speak with the patient privately and she does not leave the room, he may motion her out of the room and communicate his wishes to her kindly. It would be discourteous to ask her to leave in the presence of the patient. However, after she is out of the room it is advisable for him to inform the patient that he did this in order that they might converse in privacy.

Generally, nurses have been taught to respect the religious convictions of their patients and will do what they can to make the minister feel welcome There are, of course, some who assume a very possessive attitude toward the patient and try to keep everyone out of the sickroom. This type of nurse, however, is not common today.

Kind and Courteous

The nurse will expect the minister to be kind and courteous. But, there may be an occasion when a minister may not understand why he is being asked to wait for his visit to the parishioner. In one instance a pastor came to visit a woman patient at about 9:30 A.M. He was in a hurry. When the head nurse told him that it would be about ten minutes before he could see her he became angry. Telling her that his time is valuable also, he left. The nurse was quite disturbed over it. She was also at fault because she did not tell him that they were in the process of dressing the patient's wound. It should be stated that such incidents happen rarely because ministers are usually kind and courteous and nurses respect them for it.

Confidential

In relation to the nurse, she will expect the minister to regard as confidential anything that she might share with him regarding the patient. If she tells him that the patient is unhappy and uncooperative, she will not appreciate it if he unwittingly or purposely conveys to the sick one that the nurse has shared this with him. This pertains to anything of a confidential nature that she might tell the pastor. This confidence indicates that the nurse considers him to be an important part of the team.

PART II

THE PASTORAL MINISTRY

TO THE SICK

FOUR

SICKNESS

in VARIOUS

LIFE STAGES

When to Call

A minister's call is usually appreciated. It will be more valued if he can do it when it is convenient for the patient, other than in emergencies, or if he is leaving the city and has only a limited time in which to make the call. In emergencies or at the time of death the pastor will be welcome at any time of the day or the night.

Patients are usually "busy" until about ten o'clock in the morning. From then until noon seems to be the best time for the minister to call. After the noon meal, the patient usually prefers to rest for a while. The minister may call during the afternoon hours. However, other visitors usually call at that time also. Some ministers find it convenient for themselves and the patient to call in the evening between seven and eight o'clock. If the patient is a married woman this may give him an opportunity to converse with her husband. Except when the patient is critically sick it is not advisable to call after eight in the evening because the patient may be weary or need special care before retiring for the night.

Meal time should definitely be avoided in making sick calls. Most people do not like to be interrupted while they are eating. This pertains even more so with older people who can become quite disturbed if the meal must be postponed or if the food gets cold while the minister visits.

In the maternity division of the hospital the best time to call is between 11:00 and 12:00 A.M. The mother has usually taken care of the baby and herself and the doctor has been there. After 4:00 P.M. the mother will usually be "busy" with her own personal needs. If she is nursing the baby when he calls, she may be embarrassed if he stays. In any event he should be hesitant about visiting a mother while she is nursing her baby.

If the patient is in the home and the minister has any doubts about the convenience of his visit he may call by phone and ascertain when he should come. His most effective calls will be made if he can do it at the convenience of the patient.

Getting into the Sickroom

A member of the family will usually conduct him to the sick-room after he has removed his coat. Upon entering the sickroom he may shake hands if the patient extends his hand as he approaches. This is mentioned because it may cause the patient pain to shake hands.

He must be careful not to jar the bed and may sit down if he is invited to do so. In sitting he should be in such a position that the patient can, with comfort, see his face. However, he should exercise reasonable precautions against contagion from the breath of the one who is sick.

Achieving Privacy

Achieving privacy with the patient in the home might prove to be a problem. He may want a member of the family to be present when he is quite certain that the parishioner does not have anything to confide in him. However, on this score he can never be certain. Perhaps, if he preached occasionally about the significance of the pastoral sick call, this consideration might be firmly impressed upon his people. He may mention human reluctance to discuss our inner-most religious stresses even with our loved ones and how these weigh upon the soul. He may emphasize the therapeutic values of confession and repentance that one may want to share only with God through His representative.

On other occasions he may alert a member of the family on the need for privacy before entering the room. In a kindly manner he may explain to the attending member of the family that out of love and concern for the patient he would appreciate a few minutes with the patient alone to speak about spiritual things.

The minister's wife must not accompany him when he calls upon the sick any more than a doctor's wife goes along with her husband when he makes his calls.

When to Pray

Members of certain denominations expect the minister to pray with them during his visit or just before he departs. They would feel neglected if he did not. Ordinarily those clergymen have no problem over whether or not to pray with the patient except when other visitors are present who could disturb the spiritual atmosphere. In the latter situation he must be guided by his own sense of propriety.

In those denominations in which it is not expected of the pastor to pray, the patient will indicate in some manner or other that prayer is desired. An expression such as, "Pray for me," leaves no doubt about it. Or, "I will appreciate your prayers," or "Please remember me in your prayers," are indications that the patient wants the minister to pray with him.

When the patient folds his hands as the pastor is about to leave, prayer is desired. When there is a doubt about it in the pastor's mind, he may resolve it by saying, "I will remember you in my prayers." If the patient responds by saying, "Please do," the natural sequence would be for the minister to add, "Would you like for me to pray with you now?" In almost all situations a parishioner who is sick will appreciate a prayer by the clergyman.

In other delicate situations, at the conclusion of the call, the minister may ask kindly if the patient would like for him to offer a prayer.

I have found it to be helpful to ask patients who specifically request me to pray with them if there are any petitions that should be included. Many respond with requests for prayer that will be enlightening to the pastor and of special benefit for the one who is sick. Such requests also help the pastor to understand some of the specific needs of the parishioner.

How to Leave

When the pastor indicates that the call is concluded by saying, "I must be going now," he should go, unless the patient indicates that there is something more that he wishes to talk over with the minister. There is scarcely anything more annoying than for a visitor to announce that he is leaving and then does not do it. The conversation lags, neither one knows quite what to say. The patient does not want to offend the pastor by saying, "You said that you are leaving—please do it." I am sure we have all been plagued at times with people who seem to be unable to conclude a conversation and leave. The pastor does not want this impasse to ruin his call.

Evaluating the Call

Occasionally the minister may want to evaluate a call that he has made after he returns to his study. The following questions may guide him in ascertaining how helpful and permissive he has been.

1. When I made the call, was it convenient for the patient or did I do it when it was convenient for me?
2. Was I welcomed? How?
3. How much of the conversation centered about me? One half— one fourth—practically none.
4. How much talking did I do? One half—one fourth—practically none.
5. Did I correctly time the length of my call? Too long—too short— about right.
6. What did we talk about? What I wanted to talk about—What the patient wanted to talk about.
7. When the conversation lagged did I know that it was time to leave? Did I continue to sit and hunt for something to say?
8. In the conversation did I criticize the patient's doctor—nurse— hospital—the medical care—relatives?
9. Did the patient indicate that I should read from the Scripture— Pray?
10. When I started to leave, did I go—stand and talk five minutes longer—hold the door open a while—whisper outside the door?
11. Did the patient thank me and ask me to come again?

12. Was the call helpful to the patient? How?
13. What are the patient's spiritual needs?
14. How can these be met?

The Sick Child

Every normal child wants to feel secure and be loved. The kind of care or treatment that the child receives in the home and in the church should help him to feel comfortably secure in this world. Anything that disturbs the child's comfort or his feelings of security will cause tensions and sickness may be quite disturbing. Any sickness that causes pain, or places the child in unfamiliar surroundings, or parts him from his mother will be disturbing. An overly anxious mother or other relative may cause the youngster to be afraid by the display of anxiety, for the child will wonder why the older one is so overly distraught.

Children also want to be accepted by other children. One who happens to be physically larger or smaller than others of the same age group may be rejected by playmates. Children can be quite cruel to one another, more so to a child with a handicap.

The Handicapped Child

A lovely, blonde, eight-and-a-half-year-old girl conversed with me quite freely about this. Although physically well-developed for her age, she had difficulty with her right arm and hand. In reaching for an object she was likely to miss it for two or three tries. I found her patiently attempting to dress her doll.

"You have a pretty doll," I said. "Have you named her?"

"Her name is Susie," she said, looking up briefly from the bed upon which she was sitting.

"So you like the name Susie," I commented.

"Uh-huh," was her brief reply as she fondly adjusted the dress on her doll.

"Why did you name her Susie?" I asked.

"'Cause Susie likes me and don't make fun of me," she explained.

"Who is Susie?" I asked.

"Susie is my friend in school," she answered, admiring her doll. "The other children laugh at me but Susie don't. She plays with me. She's my very, very best friend."

"You say that other children laugh at you?" I asked.

"But they won't anymore when the doctor makes me well," she added confidently.

This child was already concerned about what others thought of her at that tender age. At the same time she was adjusting to it without expressing much hostility toward the unkind children. She seemed to feel that her handicap would elicit ridicule and accepted it, hoping that when she was well other children would have no reason to laugh at her.

A Boy of Fourteen

A boy, fourteen, was recovering from an appendectomy. He was sitting on the bed assembling plastic automobiles.

"How are you this morning?" I said.

"O.K. I guess," he said. "Better . . . but I'm hungry."

"Don't you get enough to eat?" I asked.

"At home I can eat between meals . . . but here I'm on a liquid diet," he explained.

"Is that so? Why?" I asked.

"It's on account of my operation. Appendicitis," he said.

"I understand," I commented. "What grade will you be in this fall?" I asked.

"In the ninth . . . in . . . High School," he answered, putting wheels on the car.

"I guess you're looking forward to that," I commented. "What are you planning on doing this summer?"

"Mostly swim, I guess," he said, "and some baseball and I'll help Mom around the house."

"Have you thought about what you want to do after you graduate from High School?" I asked.

"Yes, I have," he said looking up. "Right now I think I'd like to be a mechanic."

"I notice you're working on automobiles," I commented. "Do you attend a Sunday School, also?"

"Yes, I do," he responded. "I go to the E.U.B. Church. I've gone there as long as I can remember. I like going to Sunday School and church, and I like the minister. He knows everybody. I'd like to be like him."

"Have you ever considered going into the ministry?" I asked.

"Uh-huh," he said. "There are things about it I'd like. But I'd have to go to school for a long time. And it depends on whether the Lord would call me. Our minister said that a preacher has to be called by the Lord."

"What does he mean by being called by the Lord?" I asked.

"I really don't know," he answered frankly. "I've thought about that and I wonder just how the Lord does it. He has never explained that."

"You think that he may mean that if you feel that you can do the most good with your life as a minister, that that means that the Lord has called you?" I asked.

"I've never thought about it like that," he said. "Maybe that's what he means. I guess I ought to ask him."

"Why don't you do that?" I commented as I started to leave.

"Good-bye," he said, "and thanks. Come back again."

This lad has been thinking about the ministry as a vocation and he is not too young to make that decision. Many decide for the ministry at the age when they are confirmed or join a church. I will call his pastor and share with him the knowledge that this lad is interested in the ministry.

A Nine-Year-Old Girl

A nine-year-old, dark-haired girl who knew that I was a minister because she heard a nurse call me Chaplain when I came into the room told me that she had rheumatic fever.

"Whom do you miss most while you're here in the hospital?" I asked.

"My brother," she responded instantly.

"Is he older or younger than you?"

"He's older," she explained. "He's, let me see . . . he's going to be ten. We play together."

"You do?" I asked. "What do you play mostly?"

"When I get a present, he plays with it and we play house, too," she answered.

"I guess you are the daddy and he is the momma," I said.

"No, no, no," she laughed. "I'm the momma and he's the daddy."

"Why don't you let him be the momma?" I asked.

"He can't be the momma," she said with sense, " 'cause he's a boy. He has to be the daddy. . . . I have other boyfriends, too."

"You have?" I commented. "Who are they?"

"I have three boyfriends, Harold and John and Kenneth."

"Who is Harold?"

"Harold is my brother, John comes to play with him and Kenneth is my doctor. He's my boyfriend 'cause he said that I'm his sweetheart," she explained.

"So you have three boyfriends."

"Want to see my pretty cards?" she asked brightly.

"I'd like to see them," I said.

She searched among her paper dolls, scraps of paper, etc. and found three cards. One was from her Sunday School teacher, one from her school teacher and the third, she said, was from neighbors. She asked me to read the cards, which I did. No doubt she had heard them a number of times.

The next day when I came into the room I said, "Good morning."

"Oh, hello," she smiled.

"I see your partner went home. Have you another?" I asked.

"Yes," she said, "but she went to be X-rayed."

"What are you going to do today?" I asked.

"I'm going to write thank-you cards for the cards I got and for these dolls," she said, and pointed to two small dolls.

"You received a card from your Sunday School teacher," I said. "Where do you attend Sunday School?"

"At St. _____. My minister was here to see me yesterday," she explained.

"So you enjoy your Sunday School and like your minister," I said.

"Yes, and Sunday School is fun," she said.

"Do you learn anything there?" I asked.

"Oh, yes," she brightened. "We learn about Jesus, and Bible verses, and we pray and sing songs."

"So there you learn to love Jesus, is that right?" I asked.

"Yes," she said, "and God, too. Jesus and God. They're just about the same, you know. Jesus is God's baby and He grew up and loves children."

"How right you are," I could not help but comment. "I've enjoyed talking with you."

As I turned to leave, she said, "I like you, too. Will you come back?"

"I certainly will," I assured her.

Conversing with the Child

When a pastor visits and a parent is in the room, the adults usually carry on the conversation. If the pastor does speak to the child and ask a question, the mother usually answers it and the child has no opportunity to express itself. If the child is in a hospital, the morning hours from ten to twelve are the best for the pastor to call if he wishes to speak with the child alone. Another opportune time may be from four to five in the afternoon.

It takes so little to make a sick child happy. Cards are sincerely appreciated, especially pretty ones. A child usually does not appreciate humorous cards. A piece of chewing gum taped to a card, or a "life saver," or a dime or a balloon will long be remembered. A youngster knows nothing about monetary values and cares less. A big, beautiful doll may remain untouched in its box on the window ledge while an inexpensive, small "rag doll" is cuddled and loved.

Boys appreciate toys they can make with their hands. Smaller ones, ages three to eight, appreciate about the same things girls do of that same age. The pastor may establish a lasting rapport through his interest in and friendliness to a child who is sick. An inexpensive gift such as a package of chewing gum, etc. will delight a child. In this respect the thoughtful pastor can win a child's love and establish a lasting rapport. However, if the child is diabetic the pastor should avoid giving sweets.

The Incapacitated Adolescent

Adolescents can usually take ordinary sickness in their stride without undue anxiety unless the disease or injury incapacitates the youth over a longer period of time. A broken bone, rheumatic fever, or any kind of infection that is slow in healing may cause anxiety.

Most adolescents worry about school studies because they fear they may not pass the courses. If the sickness is an injury, the adolescent girl will be concerned whether there will be a scar to mar her face or figure. Adolescents crave to be accepted by their age group.

Incapacitated adolescent boys worry about autoeroticism. Almost all of them relieve sexual tensions manually when the need becomes urgent. In the hospital the boy worries about having an erection and emissions in his sleep and until that happens and causes no comment he may become quite tense. However, scarcely ever will he speak about it to his pastor or anyone else, for that matter, because of feelings of shame.

Adolescents are old enough to be concerned about the cost of sickness and may speak with the pastor about it. They may also wonder how this sickness will effect their social life and their grades in school.

A Handicapped Adolescent

The pastor can be very helpful to a handicapped adolescent. At 17 Sara appears to be about 15. She has honey-blonde hair in a pony tail and dark blue eyes. Hers is not a malignant or fatal disease; she was born with club feet.

"I'm glad you came to see me," she said to the pastor as she sat upright in the hospital bed. "I was hoping some one would come to see me."

"I see the other lady is asleep," he commented, indicating the woman in the other bed.

"She sleeps a lot," Sara said.

"And you become lonely," he added.

"Well," she hesitated, "yes, I do. I was just thinking."

"A penny for your thoughts," he said.

"I've had another operation on my foot," she started, directly to the point. "This one. I've had operations on the other one and it's pretty good. I sure hope this operation does it for this one."

"I hope so, too," the minister said. "I know you've had a lot of trouble with those feet."

"Not only trouble with the feet, Reverend," she said. "I could get along with the feet all right as they are . . . but it's being shunned and left out of things that is worse. Sometimes I wished I was dead. In school some of the kids made fun of me . . . I hate to go anywhere . . . there's always some kid who'll laugh. Silly."

"A person never gets used to that, I suppose," her pastor commented.

"My parents sent me to a school for crippled children, and there it was all right. The others were crippled, too, but I didn't learn anything. I was fifteen when I got through the eighth grade."

"As I recall it you did go to High School," the minister added. "Is that right?"

"Yes, I did start but it was the same old story. Besides that the other kids went places and did things but they never asked me. They were boy crazy but no boy asked me for a date. I saw I wasn't wanted so I begged my parents until they let me quit. I started babysitting. That's what I do . . . babysit, and I did have a boyfriend, too."

"You want to tell me about him?" he asked.

"I liked him very much and he did ask me to marry him but we were too young. And I told him that I want to get these feet corrected first. After that he and my brother ran around together and dated other girls. Then he went into the army and I haven't heard from him in three months. I guess he's found a girl who's not crippled."

"Do any of the 'kids' come to visit you?" he asked.

"Yes, yesterday, some kids from our Sunday School class came to see me. They're really nice to me. Wouldn't it be wonderful if I could walk like the other kids when this heals?"

"I hope you will be able to," he said, "and I'll remember you in my prayers."

"I do appreciate that," she said. "I've prayed a lot, too."

"Would you like for me to have a prayer with you now?" he ventured.

"I would," she said, folding her hands.

Evidently Sara feels that the only group who accepts her as she is, is the Sunday School class. The minister should feel that his teaching has been helpful to the young people of that class. His visit was appreciated by Sara, for she expressed herself quite freely. In a later visit he might encourage her to finish her High School education if at all possible because she seems to feel quite keenly about her lack of education.

When an adolescent does not conform to accepted physical standards for his age group, is either too large or too small, or is otherwise handicapped, the minister may be quite certain that the young person has emotional problems also. If rapport is good, the minister can be very helpful by showing that he does accept the person as he or she is and guide the youthful patient out of self-pity or feelings of rejection to a more healthful outlook on life.

Sickness in Mature Life

Most people in mature life can adjust to sickness without undue emotional stress. When the ailment is regarded as a temporary phase of life the patient looks forward to being normal again and can adjust to the discomfort for the duration of the sickness. However, even a toothache would be unbearable if there were no hope that it would soon be healed.

Any calamity, including sickness, may lead an individual from accustomed behavior patterns and cause discomfort or pain. Many persons can accept this without much emotional disturbance mostly because they regard it as a temporary divergence from normalcy. However, when sickness threatens to change ways of living for any length of time the patient may become quite disturbed. It can cause a change of roles in the home, a loss of status in the community, disruption of the family, and economic worries. As a result of these changes in living patterns, ego-injury usually ensues.

Ego-Injury

Mr. E. was a well adjusted middle-aged businessman with a wife and a twenty-one-year-old son. He served on the Board or Consistory of his church and was highly respected. At his department store his employees regarded him highly. He was never known to use profanity.

He developed a lameness in one leg which was diagnosed as sclerosis. However, he said nothing about it at the store. One day he started to walk up a stairway and fell. A man employee came to his aid and was trying to help him to his feet when Mr. E. cursed him and told him to attend to his own business. The young employee was amazed and humiliated. Mr. E. had never talked in such a manner to any of them.

Mr. E. became progressively more incapacitated until he was confined to his home where he tried to operate his business from a desk and phone in his den. Meanwhile Mrs. E. and their son started making decisions that were necessary for the welfare of the business. Trying to shield him, they assumed ever more authority. To avoid worrying him with it they changed certain policies at the store and hired new employees without consulting him. In each instance when he learned by phone what had happened he became very angry with them and "stormed" about it to them. He became quite sullen and gruff with them almost all the time.

His pastor called upon him often. In the conversations with him, his minister asked his opinion concerning church affairs because he was a member of the Board and his opinion was valued. The Board was inaugurating a campaign to reduce the church debt and Mr. E. had helpful ideas on how to promote it. Because he was incapacitated the minister thought that perhaps he should not ask him for a substantial contribution. In ego-defense Mr. E. must have surmised that this might happen so he did not give his pastor an opportunity to wound his ego. In the conversation about it he plainly said that he wanted to make a contribution for himself and his wife. Fortunately, the minister had a pledge card with him which Mr. E. filled in and signed.

As the minister departed that afternoon Mrs. E. walked with

him to his car. When they were out of sight and hearing of Mr. E., she said with tears in her eyes, "Reverend, please come as often as you can. He is his old self for a while each time after you have been here."

"I certainly will, Mrs. E.," he responded. "I think that I know why he reacts differently after my visits. But, if we talk here too long he may suspect something. Could you come to my office tomorrow?"

"What time should I come?" she asked, eager to do anything she could to ease the strain.

"You set the time," he said, "and I'll arrange my schedule so we can talk."

An hour was agreed upon and Mrs. E. came to his office. In the interview the pastor led her to understand her husband's ego-injury. He did not want to be shielded. His physical sickness had not affected his mental acuity, consequently he resented it when she and their son made decisions affecting the business without consulting him. Their love for him motivated them to do these things to protect him from worry but he did not want to be pitied. He resented having his status changed in the home and in the business.

Change in Role and Status

Any prolonged sickness in mature life may cause status and role changes. When the husband and/or father must assume the duties of the wife and/or the mother in the home, she may become quite disturbed about it. To protect her ego she may criticize what he does, not only to him but also to the children. "Your father is doing the best he can," she may say, "and you must put up with it until I am well again." Or she may find comfort in directing the household duties from her bed and become quite "bossy" and irritable with her husband.

When the husband is sick over a period of time and the wife must seek employment to ease the strain on the family budget, this again means a change of roles in the home. The sick husband may notice that his status of authority in the home is challenged by this change, more so when he thinks that the children are ignoring him or if the wife in a moment of irritation should forget herself and say that she is earning the money and should have something to say about how it is spent.

In cases of mature patients, the pastor will need to minister to other members of the immediate family as well as to the patient. He may help the sick one use his or her spiritual resources in adjusting to the change in roles or status and the ensuing ego-injury. At the same time he can be of tremendous assistance to other members of the family who do not understand how the sickness has contributed to the personality disorganization of the patient. In most instances, with understanding, satisfactory adjustments can be made so the family can weather the impact of a prolonged or severe sickness with reasonable equanimity.

Loneliness of the Aging

The problem of loneliness may be met, in part at least, through organizations for the aging in our churches and communities. As a general rule older people are prone to get together to enjoy social activities to their liking. They appreciate fellowship and most of them want to keep moderately busy. No one wants to be considered a has-been and does not appreciate it when a well-meaning person says, "You have worked hard these many years and now you deserve to sit back and take it easy." This is usually interpreted as a nice way of saying, "You are through! We can get along very well without you." The pastor will be careful not to leave that impression when he visits an aging parishioner.

Active retirement is a concept that more and more aging people eagerly accept as a way out of the dilemma of being "put on the shelf." Today most people of retirement age are capable of engaging in constructive activities and want to continue making a contribution to society. They constitute a tremendous resource of manpower that the minister can use in the church in the realm of voluntary service. Areas in which they can excel are personal evangelism and visiting the shut-ins and new people in the community. However, they will need to be adequately prepared for these services so that they will be helpful to the people upon whom they call.

The Urge to Be Loved, Useful and Recognized

The minister can be most helpful to the aged if he bears in mind that they still harbor the fundamental urges to be loved, to be useful and to be recognized. Each person has dignity in the eyes of God no matter how old or decrepit one may become physically. As long as the aging person believes that he is loved, that he can still be useful and is treated with dignity, he will enjoy a measure of contentment.

Chronic Disorders

There will, most likely, be changes in memory and attention with advancing years. In addition, often there is a deterioration of the sense organs, the eyes and the ears. The taste buds also may become less sensitive and cause food whims. It seems that the buds respond to the sweet taste with more sensitivity than to other gustatory stimuli and for that reason many older people appreciate a gift of candy.

The pastor may be of great assistance in helping some of his older people spiritually adjust to chronic diseases. It is estimated that twenty-five percent of those who arrive at the age of sixty in good health will develop chronic ailments in the next five years. As time passes beyond sixty-five the percentage accelerates until most people in their seventies and the eighties have to live with chronic ailments, some of a more invaliding nature than others. Most older people can adjust to these changes without too much difficulty, others may become cynical and disgusted with themselves. For the latter, the pastor may be helpful by being permissive and guiding them in accepting the handicap without rebellion or hostility. If he can assist them in finding incentives to live regardless of the infirmity, the older person will be grateful, although gratitude may not be expressed. In so many instances aged people forget to say "thank you." This may become irksome to members of the family but the pastor can overlook it.

With advancing years the patient may become peevish and easily disturbed by incidents that would scarcely have been noticed in youth or middle age. The older one in the home of a child may not want to be left alone and if it is known in advance that the younger folks are going out for the evening the older person may become sick so at least one of them will have to remain at home. This again, is an example of the emotional disturbance of loneliness.

The minister can be of comfort to older people of his parish by calling upon them as often as he can. They prefer to talk about incidents that happened many years ago but may forget what occurred yesterday. They like to know what is "going on" at the church and express their opinions. The minister will be permissive and let the older person tell him the familiar story of aches and pains that the patient may repeat time and again.

Mr. F. (Chronic Aged)

Mr. F. is eighty-two years of age and lives in his own home. A woman housekeeper comes in during the day to care for the home and prepare his meals. He finds it difficult to walk, but manages to get around in his home. His pastor calls upon him every two or three weeks. The following one is a typical call.

Mr. F. was sitting in a wheel chair, smoking his pipe and looking out the window. He evidently saw the minister's car approach and called to the housekeeper to admit him.

Pastor: Good morning, Mr. F.

Mr. F.: Good mornin', Reverend. Is it cool out today?

Pastor: Yes. But it wasn't cold enough to freeze last night.

Mr. F.: Well, I'm glad o' that. I don't like to see things freeze for the winter but it has to be that way. Won't you sit down for a spell?

Pastor: I'll be pleased to. I always enjoy visiting with you.

Mr. F.: And I'm always glad to see you, too, Reverend. It gets a little lonely for me now and then. But there's some people come to see me and Irma is real good to me. (Irma is his daughter.)

Pastor: That helps relieve your loneliness.

Mr. F.: It sure does. Irma wants me to come to her home and live there but I tell her there's no house big enough for two families.

I'll live here. I can get along all right and if it comes a time when I can't, we can take care of it then.

Pastor: Irma is good to you, as you say.

Mr. F.: She says that people talk about her 'cause I don't live there and I said, "Let 'em talk Irma. If they're talkin' about you they ain't talking about somebody else!" No, I'll stay here as long as I can. I do miss the Mrs. though, Reverend. Guess I always will.

Pastor: You two lived together quite a number of years.

Mr. F.: When we was married fifty years, Irma and her husband, John (his son) and his wife had a party for us. A lot of our friends came. And a year later the Mrs. passed away. I knew if I ever stopped goin' in the house I'd never go back. So I came right here after the funeral. It was hard, Reverend. Some of the children wanted to stay with me but I said, "No. You go on about your business. I have to get used to it and I might as well start right now." And I did and the Lord blessed me.

Pastor: The Lord brought you comfort?

Mr. F.: Yes, He did. It seemed she was right here with me. I can even hear her walk sometimes. It was hard and no one knows who ain't gone through it. But, I'm eighty-two now and it won't be long and I'll be there too.

Pastor: Do you look forward to that?

Mr. F.: Well, yes and no. I don't mean I'm afraid to die and don't want to. I'll live as long as God wants me to and when the end comes that will be a relief too. Sittin' around like this and havin' to depend on somebody else ain't no fun either after workin' as hard as I have all my life. But I figure livin' like this ain't no burden to no one. Only wish I could get to church more than I do but it's gettin' harder for me to get around. The Mrs. and I always liked to go to church.

Pastor: You've been a member there a long time, haven't you?

Mr. F.: Yes, I've seen it grow until now I don't hardly know the people any more. So many younger ones. Time was, I knew every last one of 'em. Of course, I ain't been there in six months now but some people come and tell me what's goin' on. They like you. The only thing they say that's criticizin', that is one or two of 'em, is that you don't preach loud enough. And I said to them, "Why don't you sit down front where you can hear. That's what those benches down there are for!"

Pastor: If I don't talk loudly enough I better start doing it.

Mr. F.: It wouldn't hurt any if you did. But don't let that worry you. Them two would find somethin' contrary to say about the Lord hisself. So, don't pay 'em no mind.

Pastor: It's been nice visiting with you but now I had better be on my way.

Mr. F.: Yes, I guess you have a lot of people to visit. Would you care to have a prayer with me before you go?

Pastor: I will be pleased to pray with you.

The old gentleman folded his hands and his pastor prayed: "Our heavenly Father, through Jesus our Saviour, we thank Thee for the blessing of Thy Presence and Thy love in which we live and move and have our being. The years pass but Thou are ever the same, Thy love never changes. We rest ourselves in Thee.

"We thank Thee for the kindness of friends, for the concern of our loved ones and for the strength of body, mind and soul which we are privileged to have as we go along this way. But, above all we thank Thee for Jesus, our Saviour, for His healing love and His saving grace. With complete confidence we can look forward to the days that are still ahead, for we know that Thou carest for us.

"Bless this home, this Thy servant, all who think kindly and with love toward it and toward the one who lives here. Keep our faith ever strong and in Thy good, appointed time receive us at last in the Heavenly Home that Thou has prepared for us, through our blessed Saviour, Jesus. Amen."

Mr. F.: Thank you, Reverend. Come back and pray with me again, will you?

Pastor: I certainly hope to, God willing. Goodbye.

This call required about fifteen minutes of the pastor's time. I have not recorded every word that was said, but rather the salient features of the conversation. The pastor's understanding, rapport and permissiveness are quite evident. Mr. F. is a typical old Christian gentleman.

FIVE

A PASTORAL MINISTRY

for SPECIAL OCCASIONS

INTRODUCTION

The Art of Reassurance

The art of reassurance is a vital phase of the spiritual ministry to the sick. The question may be regarded as the chief verbal instrument of listening and the positive statement is the main device of reassurance. The minister will use reassurance often in visiting the sick. The measure of its beneficial results will depend upon the patient's readiness to respond to it.

There are four principal sources of reassurance that the pastor can use: (1) his own positive statements, (2) excerpts from the Word of God, (3) poetry (particularly favorite hymns) and (4) prayer.

The Pastor's Words

The pastor's own words carry with them the authority of his office and must therefore be spoken with care. The examples previously given indicate that when reassurance of recovery or of redemption are spoken by the pastor without due consideration, his ability to help the sick one is lessened. However, when he can, in sincerity, offer words of encouragement, absolution, or confirm the patient's beliefs and hopes the pastor will convey the authority of his office.

The Holy Scriptures

The Holy Scriptures speak to every human need. The resourceful pastor may use quotations from the Bible that apply to the specific needs of the patient. To do this effectively, it is necessary that he know the Scripture and where to find what applies when it is needed. Many pastors have at their disposal collections of Scripture that may be used to meet specific needs. They either quote them from memory or have them typed in a small looseleaf notebook which can be taken with them when they call. Others may use devotional books such as *My Faith Looks Up*, by Dicks, or my book, *Springs of Living Water*. (See bibliography.)

Classical Hymns and Poetry

In addition, classical poetry and selections from great and familiar hymns of the church often speak to our spiritual needs or confirm our convictions. Unfortunately some of these hymn writers seem to have been quite carried away in the third or fourth stanzas and express rather morbid thoughts. The pastor will find it inappropriate to quote the last verses even from some of the classical hymns. "When my eyelids close in death" or "When death's cold sullen stream shall o'er me roll," or "Hold Thou Thy Cross before my closing eyes," would scarcely offer any reassurance to one who wants to recover or is about to undergo surgery. Hymns most frequently used in funeral services should also be avoided because of common association and the depressing effect they may have upon the one who is sick. Apart from those, there are many familiar hymns which constitute a treasury of reassuring literature.

Prayer

Prayer is usually considered to be the highest form of reassurance. That we are privileged to talk with God is in itself spiritually confirming. Through this mode of communion with God we may express our hopes and aspirations, confess our sins and failures, petition our needs and desires, praise God, declare our gratitude and experience His forgiving grace. The wise use of prayer by the understanding pastor will be of great benefit to the patient, spiritually, mentally and physically.

This chapter is not primarily intended to be a pastoral handbook but rather to be suggestive. However, should the pastor wish to use it as a handbook in his ministry to the sick, it will lend itself to that purpose. Alternately, he may use it as a guide in developing his own handbook for use in his pastoral calling.

▸ FACING AFFLICTION

An affliction may be described as any incident in life that is commonly regarded as causing suffering or grief; an unfortunate visitation. In the context of this book the meaning of "affliction" is confined to sickness, disease, infirmity or any influence that may result in illness.

The Purpose of Good Health

It is commonly accepted that any person who has good health is extremely fortunate. "On his next birthday my father will be ninety years old," a woman said with pride, "and until now he has never been to a doctor in his whole life." This is indeed a long record of good health for which one can be thankful to God. Many people regard such an achievement as enviable. Whether it is an enviable record or not will depend upon what the individual has done with his good health. In addition, since he has not been conditioned to sickness, can he adjust to it favorably when it does happen?

There are comparatively few, if any, people who do not at some time or other experience an affliction. For the old gentleman, who did not need a doctor previously, it happened in the ninetieth year of his life. The vast majority of people face afflictions all along life's way. Some make the adjustment without much emotional or spiritual disturbance. The nature of the adjustment will depend upon the individual's spiritual resources and how well he can use them in his time of need.

Affliction as a Punishment

An affliction is still regarded by many people as a punishment for offenses. Some suffering does result from personal sin and negligence. Some accidents may result from guilt or an unconscious desire either to compensate through suffering or self-destruction. However, it is fallacious to conclude that all affliction is a punishment inflicted by God because of personal sin.

It can be said that no person, with the possible exception of an innocent child, has lived a life entirely in accord with God's Holy Will. However, God does not delight in afflicting His people. Our good God is not watching or spying upon us to punish us with sickness. Forgiveness is always available to everyone through repentance and faith.

Affliction as a Discipline

Affliction may be used creatively as a discipline. There is no special merit in suffering unless one can use it constructively in life and then it is not a punishment but a discipline. The Holy Scripture speaks pointedly to this creative use of affliction.

Fear not, for I have redeemed you;
I have called you by name, you are mine.
When you pass through the waters I will be with you;
and through the rivers, they shall not overwhelm you;
When you walk through fire you shall not be burned,
and the flame shall not consume you.   Isaiah 43:1, 2 (R.S.V.)[1]

Blessed is the man whom thou dost chasten, O Lord,
and whom thou dost teach out of thy law.   Psalm 94:12

Cast your burden on the Lord,
and he will sustain you;
he will never permit
the righteous to be moved.   Psalm 55:22

More than that, we rejoice in our sufferings, knowing that suffering produces endurance, and endurance produces character,

[1] All scriptural references are quoted from the *Revised Standard Version* of the Holy Bible, Copyright 1946, 1952, by the Division of Christian Education, National Council of Churches.

and character produces hope, and hope does not disappoint us, because God's love has been poured into our hearts through the Holy Spirit which has been given to us.   Romans 5:3–5

So we do not lose heart. Though our outer nature is wasting away, our inner nature is being renewed every day. For this slight momentary affliction is preparing for us an eternal weight of glory beyond all comparison, because we look not to the things that are seen but to the things that are unseen; for the things that are seen are transient, but the things that are unseen are eternal.
II Corinthians 4:16–18

It is for discipline that you have to endure. God is treating you as sons; for what son is there whom his father does not discipline? For they disciplined us for a short time at their pleasure, but he disciplines us for our good, that we may share his holiness. For the moment all discipline seems painful rather than pleasant; later it yields the peaceful fruit of righteousness to those who have been trained by it.   Hebrews 12:7, 10, 11

A PRAYER IN AFFLICTION

Our Father, Thou didst send
Sunshine to dispel the storm . . .
As Thou hast always done.

An hour ago the skies flashed,
Thunder rolled, and the earth
Was covered with darkness.

But the storm served well;
Bringing life to withered nature
And the earth is refreshed.

The light follows the darkness,
Like Thy boundless love
That never fails.

Even through the storms of life,
And anxiety in darkness
Thy love still abides.

Whether it be sickness or distress,
That crashes like thunder . . .
All such storms pass.

And we are made richer, stronger
By the stresses of life
For we trust in Thy love.

With confidence we can look
Beyond any storm and see
The sunshine of Thy love. Amen.

▸ WHEN THERE IS MUCH SUFFERING

The Value of Pain

Pain may be regarded as a rebellion of the body against anything that would destroy it. No one cherishes the anticipation of suffering, yet it is doubtful if any who read these words would be alive if we were unable to feel pain. It is the body's warning signal. Through pain we learn to avoid anything that might injure or destroy the body in which we live. Some serious diseases, such as cancer, often prove to be fatal because there is no warning signal of pain in the early stages of the sickness.

Other diseases that are slow in healing, such as internal infections, sclerosis, arthritis, rheumatism, spinal injuries may engender much suffering. Pain is always disturbing, but more so when it persists over a long period of time and there is little hope of immediate relief.

Medication

Physical suffering can be alleviated to a certain extent by medication. On the other hand, when the disease is long in healing or when it is of such a nature that it cannot be cured, there may be much suffering that must be endured despite the drugs. The body does seem to accommodate itself to a sedative so that after it has been used for some time it loses its effectiveness. The dosage may have to be increased to a point beyond which it may be harmful to the patient. In such instances the physician may change the sedation and try another one to which the body has not accommodated itself in an effort to keep the patient as comfortable as possible.

Adjusting to Pain

When there is much suffering the patient with a goodly portion of spiritual resources is in a more favorable position to adjust adequately to the situation. Prayer may become a constant source of inner strength.

A middle-aged woman lay in her bed shaking with palsy and crippled with arthritis. When the pastor called she said, "If it were not for my faith I could not endure this. Time and again I pray and the Lord never fails me. It is just as if He is here in the room with me. He gives me strength and the courage I need to live from day to day. I know that anything I must endure cannot compare with what He suffered on the cross for me."

This particular woman has no problem with her faith. There are times, however, when the most devout believer may feel forsaken by God. There is no merit in arguing with the sick person in such a mood. He has most likely already argued the point with self and God. In addition, heavy sedation tends to cloud one's thinking. The pastor may be prepared to find a patient who suffers much in a mood of depression one day and fairly calm when he calls the next time. The parishioner may voice feelings of hostility toward God and hopelessness, and a few hours later express meek submission to God's holy will. Physical suffering and medication are known to affect mental and spiritual attitudes.

The "No Visitor" Sign

If the patient is hospitalized there may be a sign on the door of the room stating, "No Visitors." This always causes the pastor to wonder whether he should enter the room. When there is rapport between the parishioner and the pastor, this sign does not apply to him any more than it does to the doctor or the nurse. It does mean that he should check with the head nurse to see what the sign means. If still in doubt he may call the doctor himself.

When there is no response to his knock upon the door he may speak to the head nurse who may either go with him to the room or appoint another nurse to accompany him.

When there is much suffering the following Scripture selections and hymn verse may bring comfort to the patient.

"For affliction does not come from the dust,
nor does trouble sprout from the ground;
but man is born to trouble
as the sparks fly upward.

"As for me, I would seek God,
and to God would I commit my cause;
who does great things and unsearchable,
marvelous things without number
he gives rain upon the earth
and sends waters upon the fields;
he sets on high those who are lowly
and those who mourn are lifted to safety."   Job 5:6–11

For I know the plans I have for you, says the Lord, plans for welfare and not for evil, to give you a future and a hope. Then you will call upon me and come and pray to me, and I will hear you. You will seek me and find me; when you seek me with all your heart, I will be found by you, says the Lord.   Jeremiah 29:11–14

Why are you cast down, O my soul,
and why are you disquieted within me?
Hope in God; for I shall again praise him,
my help and my God.   Psalm 42:11

I sought the Lord, and he answered me,
and delivered me from all my fears.
This poor man cried, and the Lord heard him,
and saved him out of all his troubles.
The angel of the Lord encamps
around those who fear him, and delivers them.
O taste and see that the Lord is good!
Happy is the man who takes refuge in him!

The eyes of the Lord are toward the righteous,
and his ears toward their cry.
When the righteous cry for help, the Lord hears,
and delivers them out of all their troubles.
The Lord is near to the brokenhearted
and saves the crushed in spirit.
Many are the afflictions of the righteous;
but the Lord delivers him out of them all.

Psalm 34:4, 6–8, 15, 17, 19

Have we trials and temptations?
Is there trouble anywhere?
We should never be discouraged,
Take it to the Lord in prayer!
Can we find a friend so faithful,
Who will all our sorrows share?
Jesus knows our every weakness,
Take it to the Lord in prayer!   *Elizabeth P. Prentiss*

A PRAYER FOR ONE WHO HARBORS RESENTMENTS

O God, who art our Refuge and Strength: We implore Thy mercy upon all who are sick in body. Help each of us to know that we are in Thy gracious care. Bless the doctor (and nurses) and the means that are being used for this Thy disciple's comfort and recovery. Grant a renewal of courage for life's difficulties and uncertainties. Grant him (her) the power to find his (her) life by losing self anew in thoughtfulness and service. Assist him (her) in the strenuous task of replacing whatever resentment and ill feeling he (she) may have with love and good will. And we shall thank Thee for the transforming power Thou art bestowing upon his (her) body and spirit, through Jesus Christ our Lord. Amen.

Friederich Rest

A PRAYER TO ACCEPT PAIN[2]

Eternal God, whose days are without end,
Whose mercies without number,

---

[2] Russell L. Dicks, *Comfort Ye My People* (New York: The Macmillan Company, 1947), p. 8.

We lift our minds to Thee in our stress:
Make us to be still before Thee,
Make us to fasten our minds upon Thy quietness;
Give us strength, O God, for the task which is ours.
Thy servant suffers from the pain
Give him strength to endure;
Make fast his mind in Thee
And cause him to be strong in his endurance.
Thou are the water of life,
Whosoever drinks of Thee shall not thirst;
As the tired sheep drinketh of the cool water
And rests beside the stream;
So we drink of Thy peace
And rest in the coolness of Thy presence.
In the name of that great Shepherd of the sheep,
Jesus Christ our Lord. Amen

▶ WHEN THERE IS A PERMANENT INJURY OR HANDICAP[3]

An Amputation

One of the primary crisis situations in sickness is when a patient faces a permanent injury to the body. An amputation of any nature causes the patient to realize that he will never again be the same as he was previously. Any scar that will change one's appearance or a hysterectomy may cause a woman to become depressed at the realization that she cannot have more children of her own. She may also fear that because of it she may lose her attractiveness to her husband or become frigid.

Even the amputation of a small part of a finger may cause considerable concern on the part of the patient. When it is necessary to remove a hand or a leg or a breast there may be considerable emotional anguish. The patient fears not only the handicap but the reaction of one's spouse to the infirmity.

[3] For further insights see, Harold Wilke, *Strengthened With Might* (Philadelphia: The Westminster Press, 1952).

Spinal Injuries

Any serious injury to the spinal chord will immobilize the parts of the body that are affected by it. As a result of such an injury the patient may not be able to move the legs or use the hands. In these situations, when the injury is permanent, fortunately, the patient usually will not face reality at first. This refusal gives the patient more time to adjust slowly to the situation. It usually requires two or three months or more for the patient to accept that he may never walk again or use normally any part of the body affected by the injury.

Adjusting Slowly

God has given us remarkable ability to adjust to almost any situation. The process cannot be hastened without emotional, spiritual or mental injury to the patient. Indeed, there is seldom any urgent reason to speed the process. In a specific instance it required two years before a young woman finally accepted the fact that she would never again use her arms and hands normally.

Should the Patient Be Told?

In cases when it is fairly certain that the injury will be permanent the question is often asked, "Should the patient be told that there will be permanent impairment?"

The question may be answered by another query, "How will it help the patient by imparting such information? What will be gained by it?"

It should also be said that no one knows for certain the prognosis of such injuries and the power of God should not be ignored. Many people whom medical experts thought would never take a normal step again have recovered the use of their legs. Others may not recover although the prognosis is that they should.

God's healing forces in human nature take a normal course that we often do not understand. It is much better for the patient's morale if others keep their gloomy opinions to themselves for, as has been previously stated, hope and prayer have therapeutic values also.

The Resurrection of the Body

In another instance a middle-aged woman was found to have a cancer of the breast. In talking with her prior to surgery, the doctor explained that it might be necessary to remove the breast. She told him that she would submit to the operation only if he would promise her that the breast would not be removed, but gave no reason for her request.

Since the physician knew her pastor he confided the dilemma to him. In counseling with her the minister learned that she believed in a literal interpretation of "resurrection of the body" and did not want to live in eternity with one breast missing.

Many people believe in a resurrection of the physical body, and the pastor should be alert to such apprehensiveness when an amputation is necessary. He will then be prepared to reassure the patient that if the physical body is resurrected there will be many crippled or deprived people in eternity. Or, he may help the patient to interpret "body" as meaning a spiritual body akin to the person of our resurrected Lord. In doing this, however, he may find it difficult to explain how it was that our Lord still carried upon His spiritual body the scars in His hands and His side. In relation to this it can be said that there is very little that we know about the spiritual body with which we shall be clothed in the eternal life other than that there will be no physical defects to mar the eternal bliss. (Revelation 21:1-4)

When Adjustment is Hastened

When there is an amputation, the patient has less time to adjust to it. If it is an arm or a leg the patient will usually start thinking immediately how life will be without this member of the body. The first realization of the condition may be a quite disturbing experience.

"The first thing I remembered after the operation," a man who had his right arm amputated said to his pastor, "was seeing you in the room with me. My arm felt like it was still there. I was afraid to look . . . but raised my head just enough to see it wasn't there. Then you came over to the bed, took my other hand in yours and said, 'Charley, you'll be all right. You'll learn to get along without it. God will help you do it and God never fails!' That's all I remember but I'll be eternally grateful to you for it. The Lord has helped me and I'm doing pretty good without it."

Members of the Family

In almost all instances of permanent injury other members of the family are affected and will have to make an adjustment to it. The pastor will be needed to help them support the injured one with love and understanding. As the realization of permanent injury dawns upon the patient the following reassurance may guide the pastor in his spiritual ministry.

But Zion said, "The Lord has forsaken me,
my Lord has forgotten me."
"Can a woman forget her sucking child,
that she should have no compassion on the son of her womb?"
Even these may forget,
yet I will not forget you.
Behold, I have graven you on the palms of my hands;
your walls are continually before me.   Isaiah 49:14–16

Fear not, for I am with you,
be not dismayed, for I am your God;
I will strengthen you, I will help you,
I will uphold you with my victorious right hand.   Isaiah 41:10

Have you not known? Have you not heard?
The Lord is the everlasting God,
the Creator of the ends of the earth.
He does not faint or grow weary,
his understanding is unsearchable.
He gives power to the faint,

and to him who has no might he increases strength.
Even youths shall faint and be weary,
and young men shall fall exhausted;
but they who wait for the Lord shall renew their strength,
they shall mount up with wings as eagles,
they shall run and not be weary,
they shall walk and not faint.   Isaiah 40:28–31

Be merciful to me, O God, be merciful to me,
for in thee my soul takes refuge;
in the shadow of thy wings I will take refuge,
till the storms of destruction pass by.
I cry to God Most High,
to God who fulfills his purpose for me.
He will send from heaven and save me.   Psalm 57:1–3

Let those who fear the Lord say,
"His steadfast love endures forever."
Out of my distress I called on the Lord;
the Lord answered me and set me free.
With the Lord on my side I do not fear.
What can man do to me?   Psalm 118:4–6

Likewise the Spirit helps us in our weakness; for we do not know how to pray as we ought, but the Spirit himself intercedes for us with sighs too deep for words. And he who searches the hearts of men knows what is in the mind of the Spirit, because the Spirit intercedes for the saints according to the will of God. We know that in everything God works for good with those who love him, who are called according to his purpose.   Romans 8:26–28

Nor anything else in all creation, will be able to separate us from the love of God in Christ Jesus our Lord.   Romans 8:39

Although we cannot always understand the mystery of God's way we do know that we can trust in Him.

I greet Thee, who my sure Redeemer art,
My only trust and Saviour of my heart,

Who pain didst undergo for my poor sake;
I pray Thee from our hearts all cares to take . . .

Our hope is in no other save in Thee;
Our faith is built upon Thy promise free;
Lord, give us peace, and make us calm and sure,
That in Thy strength we evermore endure.   *John Calvin*

A PRAYER OF CONFIDENCE[4]

O Lord, thou art ever near,
Thou knowest our thoughts afar off.
When we are perplexed, worried or anxious,
Thou knowest it altogether.

Thou art the one who never fails;
In Thee do we trust.
Look Thou in mercy upon us now
And deliver us out of our distress.

Grant, O Lord, that we may pass
Through this experience with strength and courage.
Dispel fears with the assurance that all things
Work together for good to them that love Thee.

"Weeping may endure for a night,
But joy cometh in the morning";
We shall yet praise Thy holy name
For all Thy goodness and mercy toward us.   Amen

AN INTERCESSION[5]

Eternal Father in heaven, in whose hands our lives are held,
we thank Thee that we may cast our cares upon Thee, and that
Thou carest for each of us, even as a shepherd cares for his sheep.
Be with . . . . and assure him (her) that nothing shall ever
separate him (her) from Thy love. Bless the means that are being
used for his (her) health, and continue Thy gracious work, that all

---

[4] Carl J. Scherzer, *Springs of Living Water* (Philadelphia: The Westminster
Press, 1951. Copyright 1951 by W. L. Jenkins), p. 34.

[5] From Friedrich Rest, *Worship Services for Church Groups* (Philadelphia:
The Christian Education Press, 1962), p. 71.

things may work together for good. Through Jesus Christ our Lord, we pray.   Amen

▶   FACING AN OPERATION

Russell Dicks has wisely said that from the patient's point of view there is no "minor" operation. When the physician says that surgery is necessary, most patients will accept the doctor's advice and accede to it. However, in most cases there is some apprehension about it. When there is much tension the patient may ask the physician for time "to think about it."

When the Minister Is Asked to Decide

When the pastor calls, the patient may share with him what the physician has said and ask his opinion. "I just don't know what to do, Reverend. Do you think I should let the doctor perform this operation?"

The pastor must be very cautious in answering this question. When it was asked of one minister, he replied quite frankly, "I am sorry that I cannot answer your question. You are the one who must decide this and no one should make the decision for you."

"But I need your help in deciding," the middle-aged widow insisted in the presence of her unmarried daughter.

"I will consult with the physician," the pastor said, "and see what he has to say about it. If I may use your phone I'll try to talk with him now."

He used the phone in the parishioner's home and fortunately the doctor was available. If he could not have reached the doctor he was going to reserve his opinion until he could talk with him.

The physician shared with him that it was a serious gall bladder condition growing progressively worse. He was confident that she would become critically sick in a very short time if the operation was not performed within a day or two. If the surgery was postponed any longer the gall bladder would rupture and the woman would become fatally sick. "This is necessary surgery, Reverend," he said, "and the sooner it is done the better."

After the conversation the pastor reiterated to both the mother and the daughter what the physician had said. At the same time he was cautious not to advise her to have the surgery. His conclusion was, "This is what the physician advised. I trust the doctor's judgment as he is thoroughly competent. The decision must be yours, but I am sure you would be wise to follow his advice."

The operation was performed, but there were many complications and the patient did not survive. On the tenth day after the surgery she passed away. The minister was thankful that the Spirit led him to proceed with caution. If he had advised her to undergo the surgery, the daughter would most likely have blamed him for it.

In this instance the physician knew that the patient could not survive without the operation and that even then she had a slim chance to recover. The minister is not a physician and is not qualified to advise a parishioner either to submit to surgery or not to. In this instance, the minister proceeded wisely when the widow and her daughter insisted that he tell them what to do.

Apprehensiveness

Most people are apprehensive when they face surgery; more so today than in recent years. TV movies depicting tense scenes in surgery may have something to do with the increase in tensions. Most people do not comprehend how very skilled the surgeon and his associates must be to perform an operation, as well as all those who assist him in the operating room. These TV presentations emphasize the dramatic. Evidently the hordes of people who watch these scenes on TV and in the movies are not greatly affected by them at the moment, because they know that actors are portraying the episodes. But, when it becomes a matter of personal involvement the implications are entirely different. The patient quickly recalls some of these highly dramatic scenes and wonders whether he or she is to suffer the same fate.

When to Call

Patients are usually admitted to hospitals in the afternoon and are kept fairly busy with laboratory and/or X-ray technicians until about five o'clock. If the pastor can do so, he should call before eight o'clock on the evening prior to surgery the next morning. On the day of the operation the patient is usually medicated an hour or less before surgery. The pastor's visit, either prior to the medication or shortly thereafter will be helpful. On each of these visits prayer is appropriate, if the patient is a believer.

Ministering to the Family

At the time of the surgery some members of the family will most likely be present. If not, the patient will be less lonely and apprehensive if the pastor can remain in the room until relatives arrive.

When the orderly calls to take the patient to surgery the pastor may step aside so the nearest relative, husband or wife, can be with the loved one. After the patient is in surgery the minister may want to remain with the members of the family as long as his time will permit. The nurse will tell the members of the family where to wait until the operation is over so that the surgeon will know where to find them to report the outcome of the operation and the condition of the patient.

The time required for the surgery cannot always be accurately predicted. It should not be assumed that the surgeon who performs the operation in a shorter time is necessarily more skilled than another. In many instances even more time is required than the surgeon has anticipated. He is so busy that he should not be concerned about time unless the patient's welfare is affected by it.

It may relieve the tension if the pastor takes the time to accompany the members of the family to the hospital canteen for coffee or tea. However, if that is done, it is important that he so inform the head nurse who may need to contact them. She should also be informed when they return to the assigned waiting place.

After the Operation

When the operation is over, the surgeon will most likely report to the family what has been accomplished, the nature of the surgery, etc. In many hospitals the patient will be taken from surgery to a "recovery room" where experienced nurses are in attendance until the patient is physically in condition to return to the room. In some instances the surgeon may want the patient to be taken to a department for intensive care. There skilled nurses are in charge until the patient has sufficiently recovered. In most hospitals the patient's bed will be held or reserved in the room for at least a day without extra cost while the patient is in the intensive care unit.

Intensive Care Unit

The pastor may visit the patient in the intensive care unit, however, in the recovery room he can be of little or no assistance to the patient who is still under the influence of the anesthetic. If the family becomes very apprehensive while the patient is in "recovery" the pastor may consult the hospital chaplain about the sick one's condition. The chaplain should have rapport with the personnel in all departments of the hospital and can check on the patient's condition for the pastor and ascertain about how much longer the patient may be in the recovery room. This procedure usually comforts the anxious members of the family.

When a patient is facing surgery the following selections from Scripture and hymns may be reassuring.

> Bless the Lord, O my soul;
> and all that is within me, bless his holy name!
> Bless the Lord, O my soul,
> and forget not all his benefits,
> who forgives all your iniquity,
> who heals all your diseases,
> who redeems your life from the Pit,
> who crowns you with steadfast love and mercy.
> The Lord is merciful and gracious,
> slow to anger and abounding in steadfast love.
> He will not always chide,
> nor will he keep his anger forever.
> He does not deal with us according to our sins
> nor requite us according to our iniquities,
> For as the heavens are high above the earth,

so great is his steadfast love toward those who fear him;
as far as the east is from the west,
so far does he remove our transgressions from us.

Psalm 103:1–4, 8–12

The Lord is my light and my salvation;
whom shall I fear?
The Lord is the stronghold of my life;
of whom shall I be afraid?   Psalm 27:1

I call upon thee, for thou wilt answer me, O God;
incline thine ear to me, hear my words.
Wondrously show thy steadfast love,
O Savior of those who seek refuge
from their adversaries at thy right hand.
Keep me as the apple of the eye;
hide me in the shadow of thy wings.   Psalm 17:6–8

What then shall we say to this? If God is for us, who is against us? He who did not spare his own Son but gave him up for us all, will he not also give us all things with him? Who shall bring any charge to God's elect? It is God who justifies; who is to condemn? Is it Christ Jesus, who died, yes, who was raised from the dead, who is at the right hand of God, who indeed intercedes for us? Who shall separate us from the love of Christ? Shall tribulation, or distress, or persecution, or famine, or nakedness, or peril, or sword? As it is written,

"For thy sake we are being killed all the day long;
we are regarded as sheep to be slaughtered."

No, in all these things we are more than conquerors through him who loved us. For I am sure that neither death, nor life, nor angels, nor principalities, nor things present, nor things to come, nor powers, nor height, nor depth, nor anything else in all creation, will be able to separate us from the love of God in Christ Jesus our Lord.

Romans 8:31–39

In this the love of God was made manifest among us, that God sent his only Son into the world, so that we might live through him. In this is love, not that we loved God but that he loved us.

I John 4:9–10

> For he will give his angels charge of you
> to guard you in all your ways.   Psalm 91:11

If thou but suffer God to guide thee,
And hope in Him through all thy ways,
He'll give thee strength, whate'er betide thee,
And bear thee through the evil days;
Who trusts in God's unchanging love
Builds on the rock that naught can move.   *George Neumark*
(Tr., *Catherine Winkworth*)

A PRAYER OF HOPE

Our heavenly Father, as the sun brightens the earth
And gives it warmth and life,
It reminds us of Thy love,
For it is in Thee that we live and move
and have our being.
As Thou hast been with us thus far
And blessed us richly with Thy presence
Continue to regard us with Thy favor.
Look graciously upon this Thy servant
And bless all that is done for his (her) care
Guide with wisdom and skill the physician
And all who minister to his (her) needs,
Lend Thy healing forces
That health and strength may be restored
And we will never forget to thank Thee.
Our blessed Savior, watch over each of us
For we need Thee as we go along this way,
In Thy precious name we pray.   Amen.

A PRAYER BEFORE SURGERY[6]

Our Father, grant us Thy peace,
Thou who dost wait upon us when we are restless
And who dost grant us courage when we are fearful,
Grant us quietness,

[6] Russell L. Dicks, *Comfort Ye My People, op. cit.,* p. 6.

Grant us confidence,
Knowing that in this hour
And in the days that are to follow
We are in worthy and capable hands.
Strengthen him who is to operate
And those who are to serve as nurses;
We give ourselves into Thy Sustaining Presence;
I will lift up mine eyes unto the hills
From whence cometh my help.
My help cometh from the Lord
Maker of heaven and earth;
From the strength of the hills
May we gather strength
And take unto ourselves their patience;
As the shepherd guardeth his sheep,
So wilt Thou guard him,
Now and in the days that are to follow,
Through Jesus Christ our Lord.   Amen

▶

IN WAITING SITUATIONS

Awaiting Results of a Biopsy

Awaiting the results of a biopsy, or other tests, or a physical examination may be fraught with anxiety for the person. A biopsy is the excision and diagnostic study of a piece of tissue from the living body to determine the nature of the disease. When surgery is indicated and the physician surmises that the tissue to be removed may be malignant, he may want a small portion of it to be examined in the laboratory before he does the operating.

It may require a day or longer, depending upon the procedure of the analysis. The patient has no other choice than to bide the time until the pathologist can report the analysis to the physician.

When this method of diagnosis is used the patient usually knows that the physician wants to ascertain if the disease is a cancer or not. For most people there is no more dreaded word than "cancer." "I'm waiting for the verdict," is the usual expression of the patient and the term "verdict" conveys the anxiety.

Other Waiting Periods

In addition, there are other waiting periods when a pastor's call will be appreciated. Many people pass through periods of cancer phobia at some time in life, usually beginning in the teens. In former years when tuberculosis was more prevalent many people, including teen-agers, experienced periods of anxiety on that score. Today cancer and heart ailments are most feared. Consequently many teen-agers and young adults experience both cancer and heart phobias. These fears are normal experiences and the pastor can be helpful to a parishioner in the throe of either of these anxieties by suggesting that the person visit a physician. If the fear is based upon fancy it can be allayed; if upon fact, the disease can be detected in its early stages and treated. However, until the examination is over, the parishioner may suffer much anxiety.

The Minister's Wife

Especially in this area, some young ministers neglect the anxieties of their own wives. Returning home from an afternoon of calling upon the sick, the young minister may tell his wife about the ailments of the people upon whom he called. When this is done over a period of time the young wife may secretly fear that she has some of the diseases that he describes. She may be reluctant to confide her anxiety to him, for she suspects that her ailment is based on fancy and yet she cannot explain away, to herself, the fact that she feels pain. In tender moments she may summon the courage to share with him her anxiety and then say, in effect, "Oh, I know there's nothing to it. I'm being foolish, I guess, so don't worry about it."

In such instances the young minister husband may assume the role of pastor to his wife and urge her to consult a physician to allay her fears. A fear, whether based on reality or fancy is still an emotion that needs treatment. After a few years a minister's wife will probably become exempt from these psychological influences. However, there are some who never do and the minister husband may be very helpful to his wife in such a situation.

The Cancer Phobia

The prevalence of cancer phobia causes many people to become quite fearful. Any cyst, or polyp, or internal pain may cause an individual to fear the worst. There is only one way to relieve the tension or to treat the disease medicinally and that is by consulting a physician.

If the doctor suspects that there might be an organic disturbance he will want the patient to have a thorough examination. He may make an appointment either in his office or in a hospital, depending upon the circumstances. The waiting period is usually fraught with tension for it is natural for people to fear the unknown.

Any Waiting Period

During any waiting period when the patient must bide the time until the results of tests are known, there may be tensions and the pastor's call will be appreciated. If the results of the biopsy or cardiogram or other tests are favorable the patient will want the pastor to share a prayer of thanksgiving. However, until that time the following selections may be appropriate.

O Lord, thou has searched me and known me!
Thou knowest when I sit down and when I rise up;
Thou discernest my thoughts from afar.
Thou searchest out my path and my lying down,
and art acquainted with all my ways.
Even before a word is on my tongue,
lo, O Lord, thou knowest it altogether.
Thou dost beset me behind and before,
and layest thy hand upon me.
Such knowledge is too wonderful for me;
it is high, I cannot attain it.
If I take the wings of the morning
and dwell in the uttermost parts of the sea,
even there thy hand shall lead me,
and thy right hand shall hold me.
If I say, "Let only darkness cover me,

and the light about me be night,"
even the darkness is not dark to thee,
the night is bright as the day;
for darkness is as light with thee.
How precious to me are thy thoughts, O God!
How vast is the sum of them!
If I would count them, they are more than the sand.
When I awake, I am still with thee.

Psalm 139:1–6, 9–12, 17, 18

But they who wait for the Lord shall renew their strength
they shall mount up with wings like eagles.   Isaiah 40:31

But if God so clothes the grass of the field, which today is alive
and tomorrow is thrown into the oven, will he not much more clothe
you, O men of little faith? Therefore do not be anxious, saying,
"What shall we eat?" or "What shall we drink?" or "What shall we
wear?" For the Gentiles seek all these things; and your heavenly
Father knows that you need them all. But seek first his kingdom and
his righteousness, and all these things shall be yours as well. Therefore do not be anxious about tomorrow, for tomorrow will be anxious for itself. Let the day's own trouble be sufficient for the day.

Matthew 6:30–34

The writer of this hymn verse must have been worried and found
the Source of help.

Cast care aside, upon thy Guide
Lean and His mercy will provide;
Trust, and thy trusting soul shall prove
Christ is its life, and Christ its love;

Faint not nor fear, His arms are near;
He changeth not and thou art dear;
Only believe, and thou shalt see
That Christ is all in all to thee.   *John S. B. Monsell*

A PRAYER OF RELIANCE

Eternal, loving God, Thou art all healing power,
Look with tender care upon us now.

Thou knowest our thoughts afar off,
Even before a word is on the tongue.
Hear us in our prayers.
Keep our faith firm in Thee;
Remove from the mind any undue worry,
As we place our trust in Thee.
Above all else we are grateful for Jesus,
For His healing grace and forgiving love.
Help us to feel Thy divine Spirit
In body, mind and soul
As we wait upon Thee now.
Grant the courage and the patience
To accept Thy Holy Will in our lives,
That come what may, we shall always be
Content and at peace in Thee.   Amen.

WHEN CONVALESCENCE IS SLOW

Introduction

Most religiously oriented people can use their spiritual resources to meet their needs in almost any sickness that lasts only a
short time. When the process of healing is protracted for a few
months to a year or more, spiritual problems may arise to bother even
the most devout person. One of the major spiritual stresses that
may arise is loneliness. It is devastating because it can engender other
negative emotions such as self-pity, moroseness, rejection and hopelessness.

Loneliness

When the convalescence is slow friends are likely to become lax
about their attention to the patient. If the convalescent has shown
little concern for others when they were sick, they can hardly be
expected to feel solicitous about him or her. Other acquaintances
may rationalize that this sickness is going to last a long time, so there
will be plenty of opportunities to show kindness later. Since most
people are kept busy with their own interests they may consider
it sufficient to send a card, some flowers or pay one visit. As a con-

sequence, the patient may become quite lonely. This applies equally well to the patient convalescing at home. After a while, other members of the family will pursue their own interests.

The pastor can be very helpful to the patient and other members of the family if he will call as often as he can. Many patients who are in a hospital a long time have told me that they appreciate it if I have time only to come into the room each day and greet them, or wave to them in passing the door.

Self-pity

One of the most prevalent byproducts of loneliness is self-pity. The pastor will recognize this when his parishioner says, "Reverend, I've had to go through a lot. Last year my husband's mother died, as you know. And we were hardly over that when a cousin of mine had an accident and nearly passed away. After that I had that nervous stomach and you know what that can do to a person. When that was better I thought, 'Now I've had it, this ought to be enough.' But it wasn't. Now it's been four weeks since I missed that step and it will probably take another four weeks before I can get around again. I'm just waiting to see what can happen next. What have I done to deserve all this?"

This patient is dwelling upon the unfortunate things that happened as a result of her loneliness and boredom. The pastor may help her think of some of the more pleasant things by inquiring about her children (if she has any) and what plans she has for the future. In addition, he can help her find something constructive to do during her convalescence. If she can be helped to realize that she can be an inspiration to others by her concern for their welfare she will be much more patient in awaiting the healing forces.

Moroseness

Loneliness may also cause a person to become morose. A middle-aged man complained to his pastor that everyone was neglecting him. It never occurred to him that if they were neglecting him, it was because his condition had improved to the point where they no longer felt that he needed their intensive care.

Since the pastor will make many calls during a long convalescence, he will need many Scripture references. The following ones may be used:

Psalm 4	John 15:1–17
Psalm 43:1–15	Romans 12
Psalm 77:1–15	Hebrews 11
Psalm 138	I John 4:7–16
	Revelation 3:8–13

A PRIESTLY PRAYER DURING LONG CONVALESCENCE

O heavenly Father, who carest for us all with a divine love, graciously hear us as we pray for him (her) who has suffered from physical pain and other unseen causes. Give him (her) the faith and the strength to endure, and assure him (her) that all will be well with him (her) and his (her) loved ones; grant him (her) grace to forget self in daily service and thoughtfulness of others, making his (her) difficulties less important than the promotion of kindness and good will. Teach us anew again and again that it is in losing our lives in the service of others that we find our highest joy. This prayer we ask in the spirit of Him who came that we might have life, and have it more abundantly, even Jesus Christ, our Lord. Amen.   *Friedrich Rest*

▶ AT THE TIME OF A SERIOUS ACCIDENT

How the Minister Is Informed

A serious accident always is unexpected. Members of the family, in their excitement and uncertainty, may overlook calling their pastor. He may hear about it through various sources. Under the stress of such a situation many people become panicky and the pastor need not feel offended or unwelcome because a member of the family failed to call him.

In other situations he may be among the first ones called. But, regardless of the manner in which he is informed, his presence will be appreciated by the members of his parish who are affected by the accident.

Finding the Patient

To save time, he must first ascertain where the victim of the accident is. By the time he is called, the patient will either be in or on the way to a hospital. If his informant knows to which hospital the patient is taken, he may go there. If the informant is uncertain, he may call the information desk of the hospital. Usually it requires only a few minutes for the information attendant to know the name of the patient brought in. If she is uncertain, she will call the emergency department on another phone and get the details for the minister.

In the Emergency Department

When the patient is brought to the emergency department, members of his family will also come there. Before the pastor can adequately minister to them he may want to know the nature and seriousness of the accident or injury. After identifying himself to the one in charge of emergency, this attendant will likely share with him what information is thus far available and direct him to the members of the family in the waiting room.

His appearance will bring them courage and confidence although they may not at the moment express their appreciation. In other situations members of the family may literally welcome him with open arms. People react differently to the shock of a serious accident.

If the injured one is in a treatment room of the emergency department, he may, if he wishes, go to the door of the room. The doctor and the nurses will probably be very busy but sooner or later someone will wonder who he is and come to him. He should identify himself and ask if there is anything he can do for the injured one. If the patient is under anaesthetic he cannot speak to the patient but he can offer a silent prayer and through the attendant inform them that he is praying for them. Some nurses and doctors may not appreciate it, but by far the majority of them will.

In Other Departments

If the patient has been taken to the X-ray department, and is conscious, the pastor may want to go there so the injured one can see him. He should identify himself to anyone in the department with whom he speaks. If the patient is in the process of being X-rayed or examined the pastor may wait, for it will not be long until this procedure is finished. When the injured one is on the cart again he can converse briefly with the patient.

The X-rays will help determine if the injured one will be hospitalized or treated and released. It will be helpful if he can stay with the family until they receive the report of the loved one's condition. When there is an opportunity to do so he may offer with them a prayer for healing and guidance of the Spirit.

While in Surgery

If the injury warrants it the patient will be taken to surgery as soon as possible, perhaps directly from the X-ray department. In that event either the doctor or the director of nursing service will speak to the family and obtain their consent for the operation and may ask them to sign the consent if the laws of the state require it.

In this situation the pastor can strengthen them with his presence, help them to rely upon God, and encourage them in their prayers.

When the injured one is in surgery a room will be assigned and an attendant will inform the members of the family and show them where to wait until the surgeon can tell them the results of the operation.

Scripture selections appropriate for this type of situation are as follows:

He who dwells in the shelter of the Most High,
who abides in the shadow of the Almighty,
will say to the Lord, "My refuge and my fortress;
my God in whom I trust."
For he will give his angels charge of you

to guard you in all your ways.
On their hands they will bear you up,
lest you dash your foot against a stone.
You will tread on the lion and the adder,
the young lion and the serpent you will trample
under foot.
Because he cleaves to me in love, I will deliver him;
I will protect him, because he knows my name.
When he calls to me, I will answer him;
I will be with him in trouble,
I will rescue him and honor him.
With long life I will satisfy him,
and show him my salvation.　　Psalm 91:1, 2, 11–16

Come to me, all who labor and are heavy laden, and I will give you
rest. Take my yoke upon you, and learn from me; for I am gentle
and lowly in heart, and you will find rest for your souls. For my
yoke is easy, and my burden is light.　　Matthew 11:28–30

Therefore, since we are justified by faith, we have peace with God
through our Lord Jesus Christ. Through him we have obtained ac-
cess to this grace in which we stand, and we rejoice in our hope of
sharing the glory of God. More than that, we rejoice in our sufferings, knowing that suffering produces endurance, and endurance
produces character, and character produces hope, and hope does not
disappoint us, because God's love has been poured into our hearts
through the Holy Spirit which has been given to us.
　　Romans 5:1–5

A PRAYER

O Lord our God,
Thou art full of love
And we are fortunate to know
Thee as our Father.
Help us to reach with the hands of the soul
To enfold Thee to our hearts,
Where we can cherish Thee within,
Very close to the soul.

Wipe away the gloom of fret,
Brighten our eyes with hope,
Lift the heart that it may sing of faith;
And in Thy time, O Lord
Direct us out of our difficulties.
Until then, keep us serene within,
Resting in They love. Amen.

▶ WHEN THERE IS LITTLE HOPE FOR RECOVERY

Preparation for Death

The process of dying varies in length of time with individuals, but for every person death is inevitable. The minister may be asked, "When there is little hope for recovery and it is believed that the end of life is not far in the future, how do you prepare a person to die?"

Roman Catholic

In the Roman Catholic faith, the priest may administer sacraments such as confession, penance, Communion and extreme unction. The Roman Catholic priest's ministry to the sick when there is little hope for recovery is clearly defined. Extreme unction is regarded as being particularly important.

In most Protestant denominations there are no set rites or sacraments that a minister should utilize. With some, it is commonly accepted that Holy Communion or anointing with oil may be used as a preparation for death. However, as in the Roman Catholic beliefs, this sacrament and the rite of anointing also have therapeutic implications and may be utilized to prepare one spiritually either for life or for death.

In reply to the inquiry stated previously, it may be said that in the last analysis a clergyman cannot prepare anyone to die. The manner in which the person has lived and his religious beliefs are his preparation for dying. The pastoral office may be used to assist the individual in using his spiritual resources for the conclusion of his earthly life.

Voluntary Confession

In his ministry the pastor may be permissive, so the patient may express to him any feelings of anxiety or guilt or fear or remorse. When these are expressed the patient may be given opportunity to discuss their causes with the pastor.

Voluntary confession has therapeutic value for the soul and opens the way for a renewed experience of God's grace through our Lord. Since Protestant and Jewish churches do not require confession, it is extremely important that these clergymen permit a patient who wants to, to confess. Humility is a virtue and the patient with a quickened conscience may want to give expression to his feelings of unworthiness in the presence of God.

In such a situation the pastor may also exercise humility and withdraw more and more of self in the conversation and permit the spirit of God to have its way in the patient's life through the reassurance that he may offer from the Word of God with prayer, sacrament and rite.

Holy Communion and Anointing

Holy Communion may help the patient give expression to his religious beliefs and satisfy his desire for closer fellowship with God. In some denominations the rite of anointing may serve the same purposes.

The Needs of the Family

The pastor will need to adjust his ministry to the needs of the patient. There can be no set formula. The age, the type of disease, and the attitude of the parishioner will guide him. At the same time, he will be mindful of the members of the family who, in instances where there is little hope for recovery, often identify their spiritual needs with those of the loved one.

The pastor may assist or support members of the family in their attitudes. They may use the experience to confirm their own spiritual resources which, in turn, will assist them in their love and care for the patient and engender a measure of emotional and mental stability throughout the period of the sickness.

In many instances family members may not want the patient to know that there is little hope for recovery. Under such conditions the pastor may not violate their wishes without incurring their displeasure. Experience teaches that most seriously sick people do sooner or later realize that they may not recover. When that happens the patient may want to talk about it and it will not be helpful to say, "You mustn't talk like that. You're going to be around here a long time and may outlive all of us."

When One Wishes to Discuss Death

Life is uncertain for all people and when any person wishes to speak about death and the life beyond it, there are usually reasons for it that should be expressed. A spiritually mature person may want to witness to the faith. Many religious people, when they are hopelessly sick or aged and weary, anticipate release from the burden of the flesh and desire to be with the Lord. As one who looks forward to a journey to see a loved one, and enjoys talking about it, many for whom there is little hope for recovery may desire to discuss their spiritual venture with the pastor.

When the Patient Is Unconscious

When the patient is unconscious it must not be assumed that he cannot hear or comprehend what is being said. The pastor may minister under the assumption that he can hear and read a comforting passage from the Scripture and speak a prayer. At the same time his ministry will confirm the faith of the loved ones who may be present in the room.

When Death Occurs

If the dying one is in a hospital when the end approaches, a nurse and a doctor may be present in the room also. The time has come when they can no longer help the patient physically and the pastor need not feel that his presence or his ministry is in any way

inferior to what they are doing for the dying one. They, too, may
appreciate his presence during those tense moments. When the
physician folds his stethoscope, and turns to the loved ones, his
expression will tell them what they are expecting and the loved
ones will probably give vent to their restrained emotions with
weeping. At that time a prayer commending the soul of the loved
one to the care of God is appropriate and comforting.

Some Scripture selections which may be used as reassurance
when there is little hope for recovery are the following:

The Lord is my shepherd, I shall not want;
he makes me lie down in green pastures.
He leads me beside still waters;
he restores my soul.
He leads me in paths of righteousness
for his name's sake.
Even though I walk through the valley of the
shadow of death,
I fear no evil;
for thou art with me;
Thy rod and thy staff,
they comfort me.
Thou preparest a table before me
in the presence of my enemies;
Thou anointest my head with oil,
my cup overflows.
Surely goodness and mercy shall follow me
all the days of my life;
and I shall dwell in the house of the Lord
forever.   Psalm 23

Incline thy ear, O Lord, and answer me,
for I am poor and needy.
Preserve my life, for I am godly;
save thy servant who trusts in thee.
Thou art my God; be gracious to me, O Lord,
for to thee do I cry all the day.
Gladden the soul of thy servant,
For to thee, O Lord, do I lift up my soul,

For thou, O Lord, art good and forgiving,
abounding in steadfast love to all who call on thee.
Give ear, O Lord, to my prayer;
hearken to my cry of supplication.
In the day of my trouble I call on thee
for thou dost answer me.   Psalm 86:1–7

And the ransomed of the Lord shall return,
and come to Zion with singing,
with everlasting joy upon their heads;
they shall obtain joy and gladness,
and sorrow and sighing shall flee away.   Isaiah 35:10

My sheep hear my voice, and I know them, and they follow me;
and I give them eternal life, and they shall never perish, and no one
shall snatch them out of my hand.   John 10:27–28

Reliance upon God is expressed in the beautiful verses of
"Jesus, Lover of My Soul":

Other refuge have I none;
Hangs my helpless soul on Thee;
Leave, ah! leave me not alone,
Still support and comfort me.
All my trust on Thee is stayed,
All my help from Thee I bring;
Cover my defenseless head
With the shadow of Thy wing.   *Charles Wesley*

A PRAYER FOR ONE WHO IS DYING

Our heavenly Father,
As a shepherd knows his sheep and cares for each,
Thou dost know and love us.
Thou hast our name engraved upon Thy hand
Where it is ever before Thine eye.
Thou callest us by name, for we are Thine.
In deep gratitude we thank Thee
That Thou hast redeemed us
Through Jesus Christ, our Saviour.

Forgive us wherever we have failed Thee,
And grant us a full measure of Thy Spirit
That we may not be unduly concerned about anything
As we put our trust in Thee.
And when our earthly journey ends,
Grant us, O Lord, a holy rest,
And a heavenly home where pain and sorrow
Will be no more.
We would praise Thy holy name
For all Thy goodness forever and forever. Amen.

A PRAYER FOR ONE WHO IS UNCONSCIOUS[7]

We beseech Thee to comfort him (her) who is presently unconscious. By the knowledge that all things work together for good to those who love Thee, assure him (her) upon his (her) return to consciousness, that Thou wilt enable him (her) to await Thy healing with patience; Thy peace with hope; Thy house of many mansions with faith. Through Jesus Christ, our Lord, we pray.

Amen.

A COMMENDATORY PRAYER[8]

Into Thy hands, O merciful Saviour, we commend the soul of thy servant, now departed from the body. Acknowledge, we humbly beseech Thee, a sheep of Thine own fold, a lamb of Thine own flock, a sinner of Thine own redeeming. Receive him (her) into the arms of Thy mercy, into the blessed rest of everlasting peace, and into the company of the saints in light. Amen.

A Brief Service of Holy Communion for the Sick[9]

(The elements should be placed nearby upon a bedside table, which has been covered with a white cloth.)
Then shall the minister say;
Let us pray.
Almighty God, unto whom all hearts are open, all desires known, and from whom no secrets are hid, cleanse the

---

[7] Friedrich Rest, *Worship Services for Church Groups, op. cit.,* p. 70.
[8] From *The Book of Common Prayer* (New York: Morehouse-Barlow Co., Inc.), p. 319.
[9] Russell L. Dicks, *Comfort Ye My People, op. cit.,* p. 29.

thoughts of our hearts by the inspiration of Thy Holy Spirit, that we may perfectly love Thee, and worthily magnify Thy holy Name, through Jesus Christ our Lord. Amen.

Invitation or Exhortation

Ye that do truly and earnestly repent of your sins, and are in love and charity with your neighbors, and intend to lead a new life, following the commandments of God, and walking henceforth in His holy ways, draw near to God with faith, and take the holy Sacrament to your comfort; and make your humble confession to Almighty God.

General Confession

Almighty God, Father of our Lord Jesus Christ, Maker of all things, Judge of all men, we acknowledge and bewail our manifold sins and wickedness, which we from time to time most grievously have committed, by thought, word, and deed, against Thy Divine Majesty. We do earnestly repent, and are heartily sorry for these our misdoings; the remembrance of them is grievous unto us. Have mercy upon us, have mercy upon us, most merciful Father, forgive us all that is past; and grant that we may hereafter serve and please Thee in newness of life, to the honor and glory of Thy Name, through Jesus Christ Our Lord. Amen.

Here is a shorter confession that the patient may repeat phrase by phrase after the minister:

O Almighty Father, Lord of heaven and earth, we confess that we have sinned against Thee in thought, word and deed. Have mercy upon us, O God, after Thy great goodness; according to the multitude of Thy mercies, do away our offenses and cleanse us from our sins, for Jesus Christ's sake. Amen.

Prayer of Forgiveness

Almighty God, and Heavenly Father, Who of Thy great mercy hast promised forgiveness of sins to all them that with hearty repentance and true faith turn unto Thee, have mercy upon us; pardon and deliver us from all our sins; confirm and strengthen us in all goodness; and bring us to everlasting life, through Jesus Christ our Lord. Amen.

Prayer of Consecration

Almighty God, our Heavenly Father, Who of Thy tender mercy didst give Thine only Son Jesus Christ to suffer death upon the cross for our redemption; Who made there, by the one offering of Himself, a full perfect, and sufficient sacrifice for the sins of the whole world; and did institute, and in His holy gospel command us to continue this memorial of His precious death; hear us, O merciful Father, we most humbly beseech Thee, and grant that we, receiving this bread and wine, according to Thy Son, our Saviour Jesus Christ's holy institution, in remembrance of His Death and Passion, may also be partakers of the divine nature through Him, who, in the same night in which He was betrayed, took bread and when He had given thanks, He broke it, and gave it to His disciples, saying, Take, eat; this is My body which is given for you; do this in remembrance of Me. Likewise after supper He took the cup and when He had given thanks, He gave it to them, saying, Drink ye all of this, for this is My blood of the new covenant which is shed for you, and for many, for the remission of sins; do this, as oft as ye shall drink it, in remembrance of Me. Amen.

Words of Administration

As the bread is given, the minister shall say:

Jesus said, "This is My body which is given for you." Take and eat this in remembrance that Christ died for you, and feed on Him in your heart by faith, with thanksgiving.

Likewise as the cup is given, he shall say:

Jesus said, "This cup is the new covenant in My blood, which is shed for you." Drink this in remembrance that Christ died for you, and be thankful.

The Lord's Prayer may then be spoken.

The Benediction

The peace of God, which passeth all understanding, keep your hearts and minds in the knowledge and love of God, and of His Son Jesus Christ our Lord: and the blessing of God Almighty, the Father, the Son, and the Holy Spirit, be among you and remain with you always. Amen.

UNCTION OF THE SICK[10]

O blessed Redeemer, relieve, we beseech Thee, by Thy indwelling power, the distress of this Thy servant; release him (her) from sin, and drive away all pain of soul and body, that being restored to soundness of health, he (she) may offer Thee praise and thanksgiving; who livest and reignest with the Father, and the Holy Ghost, one God, world without end. Amen.

I anoint thee with oil (or I lay my hand upon thee), In the name of the Father, and of the Son, and of the Holy Ghost; beseeching the mercy of our Lord Jesus Christ, that all thy pain and sickness of body being put to flight, the blessing of health may be restored unto thee. Amen.

▶ WHEN A CHILD IS SERIOUSLY SICK

Introduction

There is probably no other phase of the pastor's ministry to the sick that is as deeply meaningful as his visits when a child is seriously sick. Parents experience a depth of anxiety and feelings of frustration as they desperately pray for God's healing forces.

When a Child Is Parted from Parents

A tonsillectomy, which is considered to be a minor operation, may cause the parents to have feelings of anxiety. It may require only a day of hospitalization and the child may be parted from the parents only for the duration of the surgery. Yet, when the child is taken from the room, it is removed from their comfort and care. They may not know the people into whose hands they trust their child, but they do know the physician and their confidence is in him.

Parents' Feelings of Inadequacy

When a child is parted from the parents for the treatment of a sickness, they will be disturbed until they can be with him again. Responsible parents know that their child is dependent upon them

10 From *The Book of Common Prayer, op. cit.,* p. 320.

for love and security. When sickness comes they feel inadequate to the situation. They want to relieve the pain or cause the fever to subside and they cannot. Frustrated, they turn to the physician whom they hope will do for the child what they cannot do themselves.

Prayer

In this situation parental urges are consciously or subconsciously thwarted. At the same time they regard the physician as the one to whom they look with confidence and hope for the restoration of their child to health again. When the child is seriously sick they know that it is going to require more than the skillful treatment of the doctor to accomplish a cure. Consequently they pray fervently to God for help and when the minister calls they look to him for spiritual assistance and hope that he will join them with his prayers to the Almighty.

The Child's Emotions

Depending upon its age, the child may understand words about the love of Jesus for little children and be comforted. Fear of unknown forces may cause a little one to be apprehensive, particularly when it knows that its parents are worried over something pertaining to its welfare. Reassurance of the loving care of Jesus may help to allay some of the fear.

Since the child can readily comprehend that the parents, the doctor (and nurses in a hospital situation) are doing things for it, the pastor may offer the reassurance that all of this is done to help the little one to health again.

Infant Baptism

Parents of Jewish faith will desire the prayers of their rabbis. If the child is an infant of the Roman Catholic constituency, the parents will want the priest to baptize it. If a priest is not available, a nurse, minister or for that matter any believer may baptize the child by using the Trinitarian formula, which is the same in Protestant and Roman Catholic Churches. Many Protestants also practice

infant baptism and they, too, may want to present their sick baby to
the Lord in baptism.

When the baby is in the nursery of a hospital the pastor may
call or talk with the supervisor of the nursery and share with her the
wishes of the parents and when they will be present for the sacrament. She will procure a small bowl of lukewarm water and clean
white napkins. The pastor will don the sterile garment provided for
him and the nurse will assist him with the child as the parents
stand in the doorway near their child when it is baptized.

At the time when a child is seriously sick, the following Scripture references may be of comfort to the parents and to the child if
it is sufficiently grown to understand:

At that time the disciples came to Jesus, saying, "Who is the
greatest in the kingdom of heaven?" And calling to him a child, he
put him in the midst of them, and said, "Truly, I say to you, unless
you turn and become like children you will never enter the
kingdom of heaven. Whoever humbles himself like this child, he
is the greatest in the kingdom of heaven.

"Whoever receives one such child in my name receives me;
but whoever causes one of these little ones who believe in me to sin,
it would be better for him to have a great millstone fastened round
his neck and to be drowned in the depth of the sea."

Matthew 18:1-6

"See that you do not despise one of these little ones; for I tell
you that in heaven their angels always behold the face of my Father
who is in heaven. What do you think? If a man has a hundred
sheep, and one of them has gone astray, does he not leave the
ninety-nine on the hills and go in search of the one that went
astray? And if he finds it, truly, I say to you, he rejoices over it more
than over the ninety-nine that never went astray. So it is not the
will of my Father who is in heaven that one of these little ones
should perish."   Matthew 18:10-14

Now they were bringing even infants to him that he might
touch them; and when the disciples saw it, they rebuked him. But
Jesus called them to him, saying, "Let the children come to me, and
do not hinder them; for to such belongs the kingdom of God. Truly,

I say to you, whoever does not receive the kingdom of God like a
child shall not enter it."   Luke 18:15–17

The Lord is good,
a stronghold in the day of trouble;
he knows those who take refuge in him.   Nahum 1:7

As a father pities his children,
so the Lord pities those who fear him.
For he knows our frame;
he remembers that we are dust.   Psalm 103:13, 14

This child we dedicate to Thee,
O God of grace and purity!
In Thy great love its life prolong,
Shield it, we pray, from sin and wrong.

Tr. by Samuel Gilman

Saviour, like a shepherd lead us,
Much we need Thy tender care;
In Thy pleasant pastures feed us,
For our use Thy folds prepare.
Blessed Jesus, Blessed Jesus,
Thou hast bought us, Thine we are.

Early let us seek Thy favor;
Early let us do Thy will;
Blessed Lord and only Saviour,
With Thy love our bosoms fill.
Blessed Jesus, Blessed Jesus,
Thou hast loved us, love us still.

Ascribed to Dorothy A. Thrupp

Prayers for the Healing of a Child

Lord Jesus, with tenderness and love,
Thou didst take little children in Thy arms,
To touch and bless them with Thy holy hands.
Wouldst Thou touch this child, we pray Thee,
That from Thy healing spiritual hands
Might flow the divine force of health.
We pray Thee, relieve the sickness,

Dispel the disease,
And cause the fever to subside.
For these purposes bless the ministrations
In this child's behalf.
Grant soon, we beseech Thee,
An answer to our pleas,
And we would humbly bow
To thank Thee for Thy love and mercy. Amen.

O Lord Jesus Christ, who camest into this world as a little child, in want and suffering, look mercifully, we beseech Thee upon this sick child. Sustain him (her) in the trial through which he (she) is now passing, and sanctify it to his (her) good. Deliver him (her) from suffering, and, if in accordance with Thy holy will, restore him (her) to health and strength, that he (she) may joyfully serve Thee in Thy kingdom, to the honor of Thy name. Hear us for Thy mercy's sake. Amen.[11]

▸ ## WHEN A CHILD IS BORN

Fear of Abnormalities

When a child is born as soon as the parents know that the infant is without physical defects both of them are relieved and happy.

"The first thing I did," a young mother confided to her pastor, "was to count the baby's fingers. And Bob (her husband) counted his toes. But, what concerned me more was that the baby would be mentally all right. Physical defects can usually be corrected but mental ones are a different matter."

Once the mother is reasonably assured that her baby is normal she will, most likely, sleep a relieved slumber, for she will be content and physically exhausted for a time.

When There Is a Defect

When a physical or mental defect in the child becomes apparent, the parents will be deeply dejected in spirit and desperately

[11] H. J. Schick, *Pastor's Manual* (St. Louis: Eden Publishing House, 1930), p. 94.

need their pastor's understanding and loving care. In most such instances the parents may be plagued with strong feelings of guilt because they may feel that something they have done has caused the deformity.

Sources of Guilt

Often some older woman has told the young wife that she should refrain from sexual play or embraces with her husband during the period of the pregnancy. During the first five or six months they probably engaged in sexual embraces and during the rest of the pregnancy period may have experimented with what some consider taboo activities to achieve an orgasm. If the child is born with a defect, they may feel that their "sin" has caused it.

In addition, there may be other sources for guilt feelings. The mother may have at first secretly resented the fact that she was pregnant and hoped that she would abort. Or, they may have discussed an abortion and decided against it.

When the mother is older she may be ashamed that she became pregnant. In one such case the pastor visited a forty-year-old mother who had just given birth. He noticed that she was reticent about something as he talked with her and was puzzled until the other, younger mother interrupted the conversation, saying, "Why don't you tell him? Go on, tell him."

Nonplussed, the pastor paused a moment before he said kindly, "I don't understand what you mean but if there's something she does not want to say that is her privilege."

"Well, then, I'll tell you," the other young mother said. "She's all wrong. She thinks because she's forty years old she ought to be ashamed for having intercourse with her husband."

Without a sign of discomfort the pastor remarked, "My mother was forty-two years old when I was born and she told me time and again that I gave her great joy and made her ten years younger."

A smile of relief came over the mother's face as she started to converse freely with her pastor about the baby. If her child had been born with a defect, no doubt she would have blamed herself and her husband.

When a Child Is Seriously Deformed

If the child should be so seriously deformed that the doctor advises the parents to place it in an institution for the care of such infants, the parents will often share the problem with their pastor. Some parents who have released a badly deformed child to the care of others have regretted it, others who have kept the child have also been sorry that they did and later made other arrangements for its care. Still other parents have kept the child and used the experience to enrich their lives with a deeper love, not only for the child but for God.

The clergyman will be careful not to make the decision for the parents. He may help them understand what is involved in either procedure and be alert for religious or spiritual stresses that may accompany their problem. When there are feelings of guilt he may permit them to share their thoughts with him and gently guide them through spiritual avenues of repentance and the acceptance of God's grace. Once the initial shock subsides and after they have confided their thoughts with him, they will be more at ease. At the same time their religious faith will engender courage and hope. Their minister can strengthen them spiritually with his presence and reassurances from time to time.

At the Time of a Normal Birth

Most births are normal and the baby is usually wanted when it is born. Fortunately God gives parents at least eight months, mostly nine, to adjust to the fact that they are going to have a baby. Those who may resent it during the first few months of the pregnancy adjust through acceptance of the inevitable to a final anticipation of a glorious event. When the baby is born, and is normal, they rejoice over it.

Some Scripture readings appropriate at the time of the birth of a child are the following:

They rose early in the morning and worshiped before the Lord; then they went back to their house at Ramah. And Elkanah knew Hannah his wife, and the Lord remembered her; and in due time

Hannah conceived and bore a son, and she called his name Samuel, for she said, "I have asked him of the Lord."

And when she had weaned him, she took him up with her to the house of the Lord at Shiloh.

And she said, "Oh, my Lord! As you live, my Lord, I am the woman who was standing here in your presence, praying to the Lord. For this child I prayed; and the Lord has granted me my petition which I made to him. Therefore I have lent him to the Lord; as long as he lives, he is lent to the Lord."

I Samuel 1:19, 20, 24, 26–28

And they were bringing children to him, that he might touch them; and the disciples rebuked them. But when Jesus saw it he was indignant, and said to them, "Let the children come to me, do not hinder them; for to such belongs the kingdom of God. Truly, I say to you, whoever does not receive the kingdom of God like a child shall not enter it." And he took them in his arms and blessed them, laying his hands upon them.   Mark 10:13–16

Jesus, tender Shepherd, hear me;
Bless Thy little lamb tonight;
Through the darkness be Thou near me,
Watch my sleep till morning light.

All this day Thy hand hath led me,
And I thank Thee for Thy care;
Thou has clothed me, warmed and fed me;
Listen to my evening prayer.   *Mary Lundie Duncan.*

This child we dedicate to Thee,
O God of grace and purity!
In Thy great love its life prolong,
Shield it, we pray, from sin and wrong.   *Tr. by Samuel Gilman*

Prayer Following the Birth of a Child[12]

O Eternal God, Creator and Father of us all,
Thou Who art our Protector and Support;
We thank Thee for a life preserved and a life given.
We rejoice in this hour and pray for Thy continued care.

[12] Russell L. Dicks, *Comfort Ye My People, op. cit.,* p. 118.

We thank Thee for physicians and nurses and all who serve Thee in the drama of creation.

We thank Thee for the safety of . . . and for the child that has been born to these Thy servants. May their lives overflow into its life and may they nurture it in a love for Thee.

Bless this baby with a strong body and a noble spirit. May it bring joy and happiness to the home into which it has come and may it grow to do Thy will, through Jesus Christ our Lord. Amen.

An attitude of thanksgiving and praise is in itself a healing emotion. Accompanying it are feelings of well-being, of togetherness with God, and friends, and loved ones. It induces the individual to think about the evidences of kindness and consideration that were expressed by others during the period of the sickness. At the same time it motivates one to manifest gratitude in thoughts and acts of kindness toward others and in devotion to God and His church.

In addition to the love of God there are many people who contribute to the recovery of a person who is sick. These include the doctor, loved ones and friends. In a hospital many of the personnel serve the needs of the sick, from the unseen people in the boiler room and kitchen and laundry to those who actually come into personal contact with the patient.

Furthermore, the recovered one would be grateful for the ministry of the pastor, priest or rabbi. His interest, guidance and reassurances greatly assisted in the personal use of spiritual resources in the time of need. Through his assistance God became more precious and helped the patient to health and wholeness.

The clergyman also craves the prayers of his people. He need not hesitate to share with those whom he visits that their thoughts and prayers are appreciated.

The following prayers and thoughts may serve as a guide in helping the recovered one express the gratitude that is felt.

Thanksgiving and Praise for Recovery

Now thank we all our God
With heart, and hands, and voices,
Who wondrous things hath done,

In whom this world rejoices;
Who from our mothers' arms
Hath blest us on our way
With countless gifts of love,
And still is ours today.

O may this bounteous God
Through all our life be near us,
With ever joyful hearts
And blessed peace to cheer us;
To keep us in His grace,
And guide us when perplexed,
And free us from all ills
In this world and the next.

Martin Rinkart (Tr. by Catherine Winkworth)

Bless the Lord, O my soul;
and all that is within me, bless his holy name!
Bless the Lord, O my soul,
and forget not all his benefits,
Who forgives all your iniquity,
Who heals all your diseases,
Who redeems your life from the Pit,
Who crowns you with steadfast love and mercy,
Who satisfies you with good things as long as you live
so that your youth is renewed like the eagle's.   Psalm 103:1–5

Enter his gates with thanksgiving,
and his courts with praise!
Give thanks to him, bless his name!
For the Lord is good;
his steadfast love endures for ever,
and his faithfulness to all generations.   Psalm 100:4, 5

For the Church and Its Ministry

Blessed God and Father of us all,
Through Thy Holy Church, ordained by Thee
We give expression to our faith.
And by it Thou dost reveal Thyself
Through its ministry of the Word,

And the Holy Sacraments and its rites.
Blessed Lord and Saviour of us all,
Thou art the Head and the Foundation
Of the Church built upon the faith of the saints.
We thank Thee for it.
In sickness we experience its fellowship,
And the power of its prayers
And the consolation, guidance and comfort
Of its ministry.
Blessed Holy Spirit of our God,
Make us worthy to be children of Thy Church.
Grant that it may ever continue
To lend its healing shelter
To sick and suffering people everywhere,
Through the Great Physician,
The Healer of Souls,
Even Christ Jesus, our Saviour. Amen.

IN GRATITUDE TO PHYSICIANS AND NURSES

I Dressed the Wound

To dress a wound is a reverent act
Done by a Good Samaritan
On the rough road of healing.
To relieve the pain of a child
Or bring ease to an aged pilgrim
Or help to heal any person
Is following our Lord's example.

To dress a wound is a holy act
Involving more than materials,
And drugs, and medicines;
Even more than skill and deft fingers.
The spirit in which it is done
Is in imitation of the one
Who made it a holy service.

To dress a wound is a sacred act;
It is not all of curing,
But a vital part of it.
God alone can do the rest.

He is the Source of all healing force
As the sage of old so wisely told,
"I dressed the wound, God cured him."

To dress a wound is a Godly act,
For the hands that apply the drugs
And wind the gauze and soothe the pain
Are the only hands God has on earth
To show His compassion
For a suffering person
With a soul that is eternal.

THANKSGIVING FOR OTHERS

Our heavenly Father, our hearts are warmed
With sincere thoughts of gratitude
For others who have in any way
Helped us through this siege of sickness.
We thank Thee for those, though unseen
And without our praise, who have
In any manner assisted our recovery;
For those who make their contribution
Through faithfulness to a task.
By face or by name, we think of loved ones,
And friends or acquaintances who have used
Their good health to be of assistance to us.
Kindness and consideration and love
Have helped to make life worth living
And encouraged us when we needed it most.
Grant, O Lord, that through Thy Spirit
We may henceforth reflect upon others
All the kindness that has been shown to us.
Use us in Thy Service, we pray Thee. Amen.

A VERSE OF ADORATION

Praise ye the Lord, the Almighty, the King of creation!
O my soul, praise Him, for He is Thy health and salvation!
All ye who hear, now to His temple draw near;
Join me in glad adoration.

Joachim Neander (Tr. Catherine Winkworth)

BIBLIOGRAPHY

Barton, Thomas, *Religious Doctrine and Medical Practice*, Charles C. Thomas, Springfield, Ill., 1958.

Cabot, Richard C. and Dicks, Russell L., *The Art of Ministering to the Sick*, The Macmillan Co., New York, 1936.

Dicks, Russell L., *Comfort Ye My People*, The Macmillan Co., New York, 1947 (out of print).

Dicks, Russell L., *How To Make Pastoral Calls For Laymen and Pastors*, The Bethany Press, St. Louis, 1962.

Dicks, Russell L., *My Faith Looks Up*, Westminster Press, Philadelphia, 1949.

Dicks, Russell L., *Toward Health and Wholeness*, The Macmillan Co., New York, 1960.

Doniger, Simon, *Healing, Human and Divine*, The Association Press, New York, 1957.

Dunbar, H. Flanders, *Mind and Body, Psychosomatic Medicine*, Random House, New York, 1947.

Hiltner, Seward, *The Counselor in Counseling*, Abingdon, New York, Nashville, 1962.

McNeil, John T., *A History of the Cure of Souls*, Harper & Row, Publishers, New York, 1951.

Oates, Wayne E., *Religious Factors in Mental Illness*, The Association Press, New York, 1955.

Johnson, Paul E., *Psychology of Pastoral Care*, Abingdon-Cokesburg, New York, Nashville, 1953.

Rest, Friedrich, *Worship Services for Church Groups*, Christian Education Press, Philadelphia, 1962.

Scherzer, Carl J., *The Church and Healing*, Westminster Press, Philadelphia, 1950 (Out of Print).

Scherzer, Carl J., *Springs of Living Water*, Westminster Press, Philadelphia, 1952.

Southard, Samuel, *Religion and Nursing*, The Broadman Press, Nashville, 1959.

Westberg, Granger E., *Minister and Doctor Meet,* Harper & Row, Publishers, New York, 1961.

Wilke, Harold, *Strengthened with Might,* Westminster Press, Philadelphia, 1952.

Young, Richard K., *The Pastor's Hospital Ministry,* The Broadman Press, Nashville, 1954.

Young, Richard K., and Mielberg, Albert L., *Spiritual Therapy,* Harper & Row, Publishers, New York, 1960.

INDEX

This bo'... may b... b... t